Clear Grammar 1 Student Workbook

More Activities for Spoken and Written Communication

Keith S. Folse, Ph.D.
University of Central Florida

Jeanine Ivone
ELI, University of South Florida

Deborah Mitchell
ELI, University of South Florida

Elena Vestri Solomon
ESL, Hillsborough Community College

Ann Arbor

THE UNIVERSITY OF MICHIGAN PRESS

Clear Grammar 1
Student Workbook

Contents

To the Teacher

Clear Grammar 1 Student Workbook is part of a multivolume series of grammar books for beginning to intermediate level students of English as a second or foreign language. Book 1 covers basic grammar points for beginning nonnative speakers of English, including the verb *to be,* regular verbs, simple present, simple past (regular and some irregular forms), present progressive, *yes-no* questions, negation, demonstrative words, possessive words, *wh-* questions, word order, quantity words, and prepositions. This workbook may be used by students who are using the *Clear Grammar 1* textbook or any other beginning grammar book. In addition, the workbook could be used by students in a beginning conversation course so that they could have written practice to supplement the spoken practice in class.

The textbook for *Clear Grammar 1* contains grammar presentations using deductive and inductive approaches to accommodate the wide variety of learning styles that exist among language learners. In addition, the textbook contains an array of exercises and activities ranging from simple fill-in-the-blank exercises to original sentence creation to error identification and correction.

The exercises in the textbook have both writing and speaking practice for the grammar points. The exercises for each of the grammar points in the textbook are sequenced from controlled (easy) to more open (challenging) activities. However, the exercises and activities in this workbook provide a different kind of practice. They attempt to simulate real language situations through the use of realia, sentence study, puzzles, and more difficult objective (TOEFL-like) exercises. Thus, the exercises in this workbook offer a good complement to the exercises available in the student textbook.

The exercises in *Clear Grammar 1 Student Workbook* follow a similar format to facilitate use by both the teacher and the student. Each of the twelve units in this workbook offers these seven exercises:

Exercise 1. Realia
Exercise 2. Original Sentence Writing
Exercise 3. Realia
Exercise 4. Game, Puzzle, or Similar Activity
Exercise 5. Dialogue and Conversation Practice
Exercise 6. Sentence Study
Exercise 7. TOEFL Review

Exercises 1 and 3 are called **realia.** In these exercises, students will work with postcards, newspaper articles, advertisements for various products, and other kinds of "real" examples of the grammar point being practiced in a particular unit.

Exercise 2, **Original Sentence Writing,** requires students to write their own unique sentences from prompts. The prompts either include specific examples of the grammar point being practiced, or they elicit use of the grammar point. For example, in unit 4 on possessive adjectives, the students are asked to write true sentences with given possessive adjective and noun combinations such as "my mother" (e.g., "My mother has brown hair"), whereas in unit 9 on the present progressive tense they are given various verbs as prompts, such as "(listening)," which would then elicit the verb form "is listening."

Exercise 4 is often some type of **game** or other **fun activity.** Learners practice the grammar point while doing some challenging activity. Exercise 4 often consists of a crossword puzzle or word search activity.

In Exercise 5, students work with original **dialogues** and **conversations.** If they are asked to write original dialogues, general guidelines or parameters are given, such as the names of the two people in the dialogue as well as their relationship (e.g., two students, clerk and department manager in a clothing store, two people at a party). In addition, students are sometimes told exactly what problem to develop (and solve!) in the dialogue. For example, the directions for exercise 5 in unit 8 on word order of adverbs and adjectives instruct the student to write a dialogue in which a clerk is stocking shelves but does not know where to put the shirts and therefore has to ask the manager for assistance. When students are asked to read a dialogue instead of writing their own, the dialogue helps learners by providing a clear example of how native speakers of English might use the grammar points in real conversation. This exercise provides practice not only in using the structures but also in listening for them in conversation. Thus, this exercise gives students practice in speaking and listening (as well as in writing and reading).

Exercise 6 is called **Sentence Study.** In this exercise, students must first read a given sentence or minidialogue that contains elements of the grammar points being studied in that particular unit. Next, students are to read four sentences and choose which one or ones are true based on the information in the original sentences. This exercise is a very important one because it not only helps learners sort out what the grammar point really means but also promotes critical thinking skills in English. In addition, it promotes reading skills in English through more rapid recognition of the given grammar structures.

Exercise 7 provides a **review** of the language points in the unit using objective questions of two types. Resembling questions found in the structure section of the Test of English as a Foreign Language (TOEFL), the questions in this exercise employ a multiple-choice format. There are two parts. In Part 1, there are eight questions that students are to complete with the correct answer by choosing among four answers provided. In Part 2, there are seven questions that contain four underlined words or phrases. In this part of the exercise, students are to choose the one underlined word or phrase that has a grammatical error in it. While students are not required to actually correct the error, teachers may find it more beneficial to ask students to do so.

Unit 1

Present Tense of *Be*

Exercise 1. **Realia** Read the following postcard from Bruce to his mother. Underline the correct forms of the verb *be.*

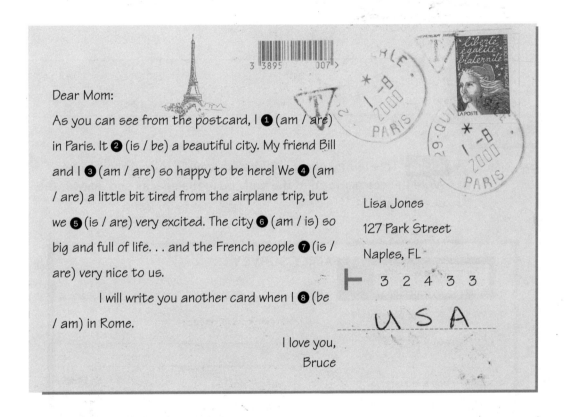

Dear Mom:

As you can see from the postcard, I ❶ (am / are) in Paris. It ❷ (is / be) a beautiful city. My friend Bill and I ❸ (am / are) so happy to be here! We ❹ (am / are) a little bit tired from the airplane trip, but we ❺ (is / are) very excited. The city ❻ (am / is) so big and full of life. . . and the French people ❼ (is / are) very nice to us.

I will write you another card when I ❽ (be / am) in Rome.

I love you,
Bruce

Lisa Jones
127 Park Street
Naples, FL
⌐ 3 2 4 3 3
U S A

Exercise 2. **Original Sentence Writing** Read the following words and write sentences using those words in the blanks. Use the correct form of *be.* Add capital letters as needed.

1. Mary / be / in Texas / with her parents.

_____

2. Thomas and Simon / be / cousins.

_____

3. the teacher / be / not / here today.

_____

4. be / the girls / home / from school?

_____

5. I / be / happy / to be / in this class.

_____

6. be / you / from Morocco?

_____

7. we / be / very / hungry.

_____

8. be / your name / Spanish?

_____

Exercise 3.　　**Realia**　This family questionnaire (survey) is missing the verbs. Write the correct form of the verb *be* in the spaces and answer the questions.

FAMILY SURVEY

1. What _____ your name?　　　　　　_____

2. What _____ your nationality?　　　_____

3. What _____ your current address?　_____

　　　　　　　　　　　　　　　　　　　_____

4. _____ you a student?　　　　　　yes　　no

5. _____ you an only child?　　　　yes　　no

6. What _____ your parents' names?　mother _____

　　　　　　　　　　　　　　　　　　father _____

7. _____ you married?　　　　　　yes　　no

8. If yes, what _____ your spouse's name?　_____

Thank you for filling out this survey.

Exercise 4.   **Puzzle/Game**   Read the clues on the left. Fill in the missing form of the verb *be* (*is, are, isn't, aren't*) in the clue sentences. In the spaces on the right, write the missing letters to give the answers.

Clue   *Answer*

1. This city _____ the capital of Romania.   B U _ _ _ _ _ _ T

2. The Hawaiian Islands _____ in this ocean.   _ _ C _ _ I _ _

3. She _____ a famous singer.   M _ _ _ _ _ _ A

4. New York City _____ the capital of this country.   T H E _ N _ _ _ _

                                                            _ _ _ _ _ _ S

5. This long river _____ in Africa.   _ _ L _ _

6. Pele and Ronaldo _____ from this country.   _ R _ Z _ _ _

7. Mount Fuji _____ in South Korea.   _ _ P _ N

8. People from Canada _____ this nationality.   C _ _ _ _ _ I A N

Exercise 5.   **Dialogue and Conversation Practice**   Keiko and Waheeb are classmates. Keiko is from Japan, and Waheeb is from Kuwait. Write a dialogue (questions and answers) using at least six of the vocabulary words below. Use affirmative and negative of *be*.

| my name | Japanese | from Kuwait | baseball | music | Italian |
| engineer | student | pizza | movies | grammar | hungry |

Keiko: _____

Waheeb: _____

Keiko: _____

Waheeb: _____

Keiko: _____

Waheeb: _____

Keiko: _____

Waheeb: _____

Exercise 6.   **Sentence Study**   Read the beginning sentences. Then read the answer choices and put a check mark in front of **all of the sentences that are true** based on the beginning sentences. Remember that more than one answer is possible sometimes.

1. Bob and Gary are friends, but they aren't brothers.
   ___ a. They have the same parents.
   ___ b. They don't have the same parents.
   ___ c. They don't know each other.
   ___ d. They have the same last name.

2. All the grammar books are on the desk, and all the dictionaries are on the table.
   ___ a. The grammar books are not on the table.
   ___ b. There is more than one grammar book.
   ___ c. The dictionaries are not on the desk.
   ___ d. There is more than one dictionary.

3. Victor is in his kitchen.
   ___ a. He is at home.
   ___ b. He is at school.
   ___ c. There is a stove in this room.
   ___ d. There is a sofa in this room.

4. Carla is a student in high school. She is an excellent student.
   ___ a. Carla is 26 years old.
   ___ b. Carla is not a teacher.
   ___ c. Carla has good test scores.
   ___ d. Carla does not have many friends.

5. The white cats and the gray cat are in the dining room.
   ___ a. They are in the refrigerator.
   ___ b. They are not in the living room.
   ___ c. They are inside the house.
   ___ d. There are more than two cats.

6. Sandra is an elementary school teacher, and her husband is a high school teacher.
    ___ a. Sandra is a teacher.
    ___ b. Sandra's husband is a teacher.
    ___ c. They are teachers at the same school.
    ___ d. Sandra's school is near the post office and the bank.

7. The blue car is $18,000, but the white car is $16,000.
    ___ a. The blue car is the same price as the white car.
    ___ b. The blue car and the white car are the same price.
    ___ c. The blue car is more expensive than the white car.
    ___ d. The white car is more expensive than the blue car.

8. Shelly plays the piano very well, but she can't play the guitar.
    ___ a. The way that she plays the piano is really good.
    ___ b. The way that she plays the guitar is really good.
    ___ c. The way that she sings is really good.
    ___ d. The way that she speaks English is really good.

Exercise 7.   **TOEFL Review**

Part 1.   Completion. For items 1 through 8, circle the letter of the answer that best completes the statement or question.

1. Caracas ___ in Venezuela.

    a. be

    b. are

    c. is

    d. am

2. Gretchen and Bob ___ friends.

    a. be

    b. are

    c. is

    d. am

3. Pusan is in South Korea, but it ___ the biggest city in South Korea.

    a. are not

    b. is not

    c. am not

    d. be not

4. ___ you from Panama?

    a. Are

    b. Is

    c. Be

    d. Am

5. The books ___ in my bag.

    a. no are

    b. are no

    c. aren't

    d. isn't

6. ___ your brother?

    a. He is

    b. Are they

    c. Is he

    d. They are

7. We ___ sleepy today.

    a. no

    b. aren't

    c. isn't

    d. am not

8. Gasoline ___ expensive here.

   a. are

   b. is not

   c. not

   d. am

Part 2. Error Identification. For items 9 through 15, read each sentence carefully. Look at the underlined parts. Circle the letter that shows the incorrect part.

9. <u>My</u> <u>mother</u> and <u>father</u> <u>is not</u> happy today.
    A   B   C   D

10. <u>Are</u> <u>the</u> teacher <u>from</u> New York <u>City</u>?
    A B   C   D

11. My <u>grammar</u> <u>book</u> <u>no is</u> on the <u>table</u>.
         A   B   C   D

12. <u>Josephine</u> and Paul Smith <u>no home</u> this <u>week</u>. They <u>are</u> on vacation.
      A   B   C   D

13. Let's <u>go</u> to a <u>movie</u>. We <u>be</u> all free <u>today</u> after class.
        A   B   C   D

14. Billy <u>not</u> a taxi <u>driver</u>. He <u>is a</u> bus <u>driver</u>.
         A   B   C   D

15. <u>Are</u> these <u>good</u> <u>grammar</u> exercises? Yes, <u>they good</u>.
    A   B   C   D

Unit 2

Present Tense of Regular Verbs

Exercise 1. **Realia** Help the people below pack their suitcases for a trip to Florida. Frank is going to school to study English. The Martins are going to Disney World. Use the present tense of the verb *need* in the affirmative and negative.

example: <u>Frank needs sunglasses.</u>

<u>Frank doesn't need a skirt.</u>

- blue jeans
- diapers
- lipstick
- an English dictionary

1. _____

2. _____

3. _____

4. _____

• a radio
• a credit card
• baby toys
• a bicycle

5. _____

6. _____

7. _____

8. _____

Exercise 2. **Original Sentence Writing** Write four true affirmative sentences and four true negative sentences about your family or friends. Use the verbs in parentheses.

(watch)   1. _____

(drive)   2. _____

(speak)   3. _____

(understand)   4. _____

(read)   5. _____

(buy)   6. _____

(like)   7. _____

(cook)   8. _____

Exercise 3. **Realia** You are a travel agent. Josie calls you for information about a cruise for her and her husband. Use the information from the advertisement and write short *yes/no* answers to her questions.

T: Hello. This is Unique Travel. How may I help you?

J: I need some information about the Caribbean cruise.

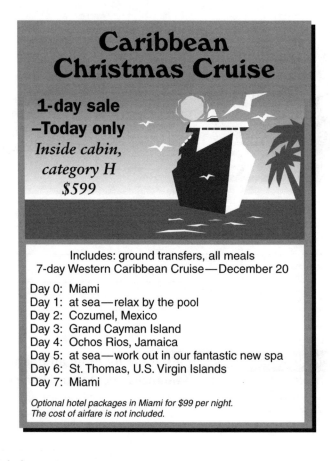

Caribbean Christmas Cruise

1-day sale –Today only
Inside cabin, category H $599

Includes: ground transfers, all meals
7-day Western Caribbean Cruise—December 20

Day 0: Miami
Day 1: at sea—relax by the pool
Day 2: Cozumel, Mexico
Day 3: Grand Cayman Island
Day 4: Ochos Rios, Jamaica
Day 5: at sea—work out in our fantastic new spa
Day 6: St. Thomas, U.S. Virgin Islands
Day 7: Miami

Optional hotel packages in Miami for $99 per night.
The cost of airfare is not included.

T: How can I help you?
J: Does the ship have a pool?

T: _____ ❶
J: Does the ship stop in Ochos Rios?

T: _____ ❷
J: Are all meals included?

T: _____ ❸
J: Is the airfare included?

T: _____ ❹
J: Do we return to Miami on December 27th?

T: _____ ❺
J: Does the ship stop in Puerto Rico?

T: _____ ❻
J: Do we get a free hotel stay in Miami?

T: _____ ❼
J: Do I need to pay for it now?

T: _____ ❽
J: OK. I will come by your office later today.

Exercise 4.   **Puzzle/Game** Use the verb list below to fill in the blanks for the clues. Use the correct form and spelling of each verb. Then fill in the answers in the puzzle.

sew	go	kiss	sing	speak
be	wash	use	cash	cry

Present Tense Verbs

Across:

1. Kim and Tom _____ men's suits at the tailor shop.

3. My baby sister _____ when she is hungry.

6. Celia _____ her children every morning before they go to school.

8. He _____ to the beach on weekends.

9. Australians _____ English.

Down:

2. Elizabeth _____ the dishes after dinner.

3. He _____ his check at the bank every Friday.

4. A tulip _____ a flower.

5. Ted and Jan _____ in the choir.

7. I _____ chopsticks when I eat.

Exercise 5.   **Dialogue and Conversation Practice** Emma and Aya are new friends. Write a dialogue using questions and short answers about their daily habits, their interests, and the things they like.

Emma: I like to play sports. Do you?

Aya: No, I don't. I like to read. What about you? Do you like to read?

Emma: _____

Aya: _____

Emma: _____

Aya: _____

Emma: _____

Aya: _____

Emma: _____

Aya: _____

Exercise 6. **Sentence Study** For numbers 1 through 4, read the beginning sentences. Then read the answer choices and put a check mark in front of **all of the sentences that are true** based on the beginning sentences. For numbers 5 through 8, read the beginning question. Then read the answer choices and put a check mark in front of **all of the answers that are possible** based on the beginning questions. Remember that more than one answer is possible sometimes.

1. Most people in Switzerland speak German and French.
   ___ a. They speak two languages.
   ___ b. They speak only one language.
   ___ c. Switzerland has more people than Germany and France.
   ___ d. Germans and French people speak Swiss.

2. I don't usually get up early on the weekend.
   ___ a. I don't usually wake up early on Saturdays.
   ___ b. I usually play tennis early on Sunday mornings.
   ___ c. I usually go to sleep early on the weekend.
   ___ d. I usually sleep late on Sundays.

3. Ben has milk for breakfast every day.
   ___ a. Ben drinks milk every day.
   ___ b. Ben drinks milk for breakfast.
   ___ c. Ben doesn't drink milk on the weekends.
   ___ d. Ben almost never drinks milk.

4. Karen and I don't watch television because we don't have a television.
   ___ a. I do not have a television.
   ___ b. Karen does not have a television.
   ___ c. I have a television, but I never watch it.
   ___ d. Karen has a television, but she never watches it.

5. Does your brother work at the bank?

___ a. Yes, he does.

___ b. No, he doesn't have a checking account.

___ c. No, he doesn't. He works at the school.

___ d. Yes, I want to work at the bank.

6. Does this radio take four type A batteries or six type AA batteries?

___ a. It uses four type A batteries.

___ b. It doesn't require any batteries. It's electric.

___ c. It takes six type AA batteries.

___ d. I think it takes six type AA batteries.

7. Do you get up early every morning?

___ a. Yes, I eat breakfast every morning.

___ b. No, I don't get the paper in the morning.

___ c. Yes, I do. I get up at 6:00 A.M.

___ d. No, I don't. I wake up at 11:00 A.M.

8. Does Kevin's apartment have 2 bedrooms?

___ a. No, it doesn't. It has 1 bedroom and 1 bathroom.

___ b. Yes, he has a new bed in his bedroom.

___ c. Yes, it does. He has a bedroom, and his cousin has a bedroom.

___ d. No, it has only one bedroom.

Exercise 7.   **TOEFL Review**

Part 1.   Completion. For items 1 through 8, circle the letter of the answer that best completes the statement or question.

1. Paul and I ___ to school every day.

   a. drive

   b. don't drives

   c. drives

   d. doesn't drive

2. June ___ 31 days. It has only 30.

   a. doesn't has

   b. don't have

   c. has

   d. doesn't have

3. I need a computer. ___ computers?

   a. Does Target sell

   b. Is target sell

   c. Does sell Target

   d. Sells Target

4. ___ rabbits eat carrots?

   a. Is

   b. Does

   c. Do

   d. Are

5. "Does it rain very often in Phoenix?"

   "No, ___ ."

   a. it don't

   b. no rain

   c. it isn't

   d. it doesn't

6. "Is Oksana from Russia?"

   "No, she's from Belarus, but ___ Russian."

   a. she speaks

   b. your school have

   c. she is speak

   d. does she speak

7. Sammy and Jane ___ meat. They are vegetarians.

   a. don't eat

   b. aren't eat

   c. doesn't eat

   d. eats

8. Every night after dinner, I wash the dishes, and my sister ___ them.

   a. drys

   b. dries

   c. dryies

   d. driys

Part 2. Error Identification. For items 9 through 15, read each sentence carefully. Look at the underlined parts. Circle the letter that shows the incorrect part.

9. Venezuela and Argentina <u>are</u> two countries in South America, but <u>they very</u> different.
                           A   B

   Venezuela <u>has</u> a tropical climate. Argentina <u>doesn't have</u> a tropical climate.
                       C   D

10. <u>Does</u> your teacher <u>give</u> you homework? Our teacher <u>doesn't give</u> us any during the
     A   B   C

    week, but she <u>give</u> us a lot on the weekends.
                   D

11. <u>Do</u> you <u>like</u> soccer? I <u>likes</u> soccer very much, but I <u>don't like</u> baseball.
     A   B   C   D

12. Sheila <u>listens</u> to tapes in her car because her stereo at home <u>is not work</u>. She <u>needs</u> to
             A   B   C

    buy a new stereo, but they <u>are</u> very expensive.
                            D

13. Cathy and Mark <u>go</u> to church every Sunday. Omar <u>visits</u> the mosque every Friday.
                    A   B

    <u>Does</u> Frazier <u>goes</u> to church or the mosque?
     C   D

14. The words "football" and "soccer" <u>are</u> sometimes confused. In American football, a
                                          A

    player <u>catchs</u> the ball with his hands. In soccer, the player <u>doesn't</u> <u>catch</u> the ball with
           B   C   D

    his or her hands.

15. *Jill:*   "<u>Do you understand</u> the teacher?"
                    A   B

    Sandra: "Yes, <u>I do</u>. But Mauricio <u>isn't understand</u> her."
                     C   D

Unit 3

Demonstratives

Exercise 1.   **Realia** Look at the picture of the bakery. Start at the entrance. Read the conversation as the owner of the bakery tells the customer about his products. Fill in the blanks with *these* or *those*.

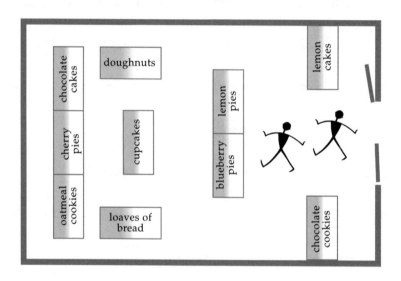

Owner: Welcome to my bakery! Let me tell you what we have today. Here are

some delicious items. ❶ _____ lemon cakes are very moist, and so

are ❷ _____ blueberry pies. Do you like pies?

Customer: Yes, I do. How about ❸ _____ cherry pies? Are they good?

Owner: Yes, ❹ _____ pies are very good, and so are ❺ _____

chocolate cakes next to them. ❻ _____ doughnuts near the

cake are also excellent. We have cream and jelly. If you like cupcakes,

❼ _____ cupcakes across the store are wonderful. We have choco-

late and vanilla.

Customer: M-m-m! ❽ _____ cupcakes sound delicious, but I really love

cookies. Can you tell me about ❾ _____ cookies in the corner?

Owner: Yes. They are oatmeal.

16

⑩ _____ cookies next to us are very popular as well. They're chocolate.

Customer: Oh! I can't decide! Maybe I'll just take one of **⑪** _____ lemon pies over here.

Owner: That's an excellent choice. Enjoy your purchase!

Exercise 2. **Original Sentence Writing** Read the following words and write sentences using those words in the blanks. Use the correct form of _be_. Add capital letters as needed. Be sure to add a period at the end of each statement and a question mark at the end of each question.

Statements

1. trees / beautiful / those / (be)

   _____

2. interesting / book / this / an / (be)

   _____

3. peaches / delicious / these / (be)

   _____

4. hat / lovely / that / a / (be)

   _____

5. those / sick / (be) / cats

   _____

Questions

6. wet / these / towels / (be)

   _____

7. that / wonderful / song / a / (be)

   _____

8. course/ for / this / difficult / you / a / (be)

   _____

9. expensive / those / very / shoes / (be)

   _____

10. heavy / these / boxes / (be)

    _____

Exercise 3. **Realia** Look at the picture of the pet shop. Start at the entrance. Read the conversation as the man, who is the owner of the pet shop, talks to the woman about the birds. Fill in the blanks with *this, that, these,* or *those*.

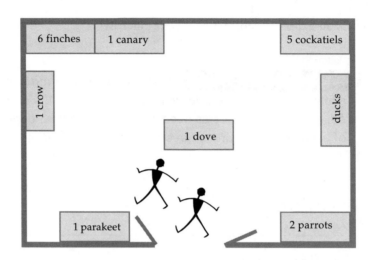

Woman: Good afternoon, sir. I'm interested in information about your birds.

Man: Certainly, ma'am. Let me tell you a little about our birds. ❶ _____ is a parakeet. As you see, it is very small. ❷ _____ is a very small bird, also. It is a dove. It will not grow to be very large. However, these birds will get very large. They are parrots.

Woman: I see. How about the birds over there? Can you tell me about them?

Man: Well, ❸ _____ are cockatiels. They grow very large, and they are very friendly. Next to the cockatiels are the ducks. ❹ _____ birds are nice, but they don't make good pets.

Woman: What about the yellow one?

Man: Oh, ❺ _____ is a canary. It sings beautifully. Its colors can change. Sometimes it's light yellow, but sometimes it's dark.

Woman: How about the ❻ _____ black bird? Is it a friendly bird?

Man: ❼ _____ is a crow. It's not friendly, but do you see the finches over there? ❽ _____ are very good birds.

Woman: Thank you so much for your time. I want to speak to my family, and then maybe I'll return with my son so he can choose a bird he likes.

Exercise 4. **Puzzle/Game** Read the clues for the crossword puzzle. Underline the correct word forms and fill in the blanks. Then fill in the answers in the puzzle.

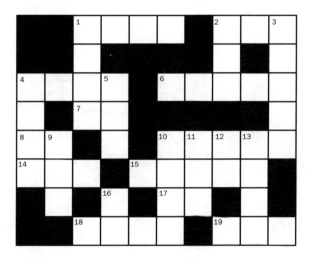

Across

1. (*These, This*) is a beautiful painting.

2. This word is the opposite of *dry*.

4. (*Those, That*) dog is intelligent.

6. (*That, Those*) new cars are expensive.

7. "Excuse me. Does this bus go _____ Houston?"

8. "_____ those cookies are chocolate, I will eat many of them."

10. (*That, These*) are fragrant flowers.

14. This word is the opposite of *happy*.

    _____

15. (*These, Those*) shirts are very comfortable.

17. This class begins _____ 10 A.M.

18. (*This, That*) star is far away.

19. These are _____ numbers: 1, 3, 5, 7, 9.

Down

1. (*Those, That*) is an expensive hat.

2. _____ is your history teacher?

3. (*This, These*) are diamond earrings.

4. (*These, This*) movie is interesting.

5. This word is the opposite of *bottom*.

9. This word is the opposite of *near*.

10. (*That, Those*) is a very good question.

11. This word is the opposite of *cold*.

12. These are the last two letters in these words: *cities, babies, cries*.

13. If you want to _____ a letter to your friend, you have to go to the post office.

16. These are the first two letters in these words: *where, when, why*.

Exercise 5. **Dialogue and Conversation Practice** Look at the picture of the party and imagine that these people are your relatives. Tell your friend about your family. Complete the dialogue with *this, that, these,* or *those* and the words in parentheses. Use the correct form of the verb *be.*

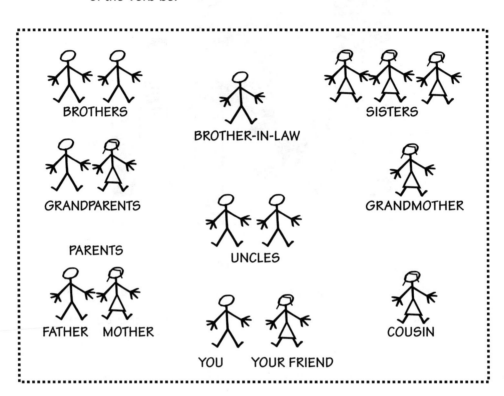

Your friend: I'm very happy you invited me to your party, but I'm a little nervous. There are so many people here. Maybe you can tell me a little about them before you introduce me to them.

You: (my parents) ❶ _____ . They came to this country three months ago. They want to learn English.

Your friend: They seem nice. Who are the two men in front of us?

You: (my uncles) ❷ _____ . They have lived here for several years. They speak English well.

Your friend: Who are the three girls over there?

You: (my sisters) ❸ _____ . They are 17, 19, and 22 years old. Do you see the man near them? (my brother-in-law) ❹ _____ . He is married to my oldest sister.

Your friend: How about the two men near your brother-in-law? Who are they?

You: (my brothers) ❺ _____ . They are older than I am.

Your friend: Who are the older people near your brothers?

You: (my grandparents) ❻ _____ .

They are only visiting, but do you see the older woman to our right? (my grandmother) ❼ _____ . She lives here. Oh! I almost forgot! (my cousin) ❽ _____ _____ . She's our age. I think you'll like her. Let's go say hello.

Exercise 6. **Sentence Study** Read the beginning sentences. Then read the answer choices and put a check mark in front of **all of the sentences that are true** based on the beginning sentences. Remember that more than one answer is possible sometimes.

1. Those are Josalynn's cats.
   ___ a. Josalynn has only one cat.
   ___ b. Josalynn has more than one cat.
   ___ c. Josalynn's cats are near me.
   ___ d. Josalynn's cats are far from me.

2. These are delicious cookies.
   ___ a. I have just one cookie.
   ___ b. The cookies are near me.
   ___ c. I have more than one cookie.
   ___ d. The cookies are far from me.

3. This is an expensive car.
   ___ a. There is just one car.
   ___ b. The car is far from me.
   ___ c. There are two cars.
   ___ d. The car is near me.

4. Kyle said, "This is an interesting book."
   ___ a. The book is far from Kyle.
   ___ b. Kyle is reading more than one book now.
   ___ c. The book is near Kyle.
   ___ d. Kyle is talking about one book.

5. These are colorful sweaters.
   ___ a. There is only one sweater.
   ___ b. The sweaters are far from me.
   ___ c. There is more than one sweater.
   ___ d. The sweaters are near me.

6. Those are beautiful fish in Sani's aquarium.
   ___ a. There isn't just one fish.
   ___ b. The fish are far from me.
   ___ c. There is only one fish.
   ___ d. The fish are near me.

7. This blue car is expensive, but that white car is cheap.
   ___ a. The blue car is near the speaker.
   ___ b. The white car is near the speaker.
   ___ c. There is one blue car, but there are two white cars.
   ___ d. There is one white car, but there are two blue cars.

8. These are tight shoes.
   ___ a. There is only one shoe.
   ___ b. The shoes are far from me.
   ___ c. There is more than one shoe.
   ___ d. The shoes are near me.

Exercise 7.   **TOEFL Review**

Part 1.   Completion. For items 1 through 8, circle the letter of the answer that best completes the statement or question.

1. ___ is an interesting exercise.

   a. These

   b. This

   c. Those

   d. They

2. ___ fish are colorful.

   a. These

   b. That

   c. This

   d. They're

3. __ are my sister's children.

   a. This

   b. Their

   c. Those

   d. That

4. __ is my favorite movie.

   a. These

   b. This

   c. Those

   d. They

5. __ cake is delicious.

   a. It

   b. Those

   c. These

   d. That

6. Is __ your wallet?

   a. those

   b. this

   c. these

   d. they

7. __ children are very polite.

   a. Those

   b. They

   c. That

   d. This

8. ___ sweater is very warm.

    a. Those

    b. These

    c. This

    d. There

Part 2.   Error Identification. For items 9 through 15, read each sentence carefully. Look at the underlined parts. Circle the letter that shows the incorrect part.

9. <u>These</u> are my sisters. <u>This</u> men are their husbands. <u>They</u> are happily married. <u>That</u> is
      A   B   C   D

    certain.

10. <u>This is</u> your hairbrush? I know <u>this</u> is mine, <u>that</u> is my sister's, and <u>this</u> is my brother's.
      A   B   C   D

11. <u>Those</u> are beautiful flowers, <u>that</u> is a shady tree, and <u>that are</u> healthy plants. <u>That</u> is
      A   B   C   D

    certainly a beautiful garden.

12. <u>Is these</u> your favorite movie? <u>This</u> can't be your favorite movie; <u>this</u> was written
      A   B   C

    before you were born. <u>This</u> movie is very old.
                                D

13. Look at <u>those</u> books. <u>Those</u> are really interesting books, but <u>they</u> are difficult to read.
              A   B   C

    <u>This</u> books are much easier to read.
     D

14. <u>Those</u> girls over there are South American. <u>They</u> come from Brazil, but <u>they</u> speak
      A   B   C

    English well. <u>That</u> boys are Brazilian, also.
                   D

15. <u>This</u> poem is beautiful. <u>There</u> are two main characters in it, and <u>they</u> are very
      A   B   C

    adventurous. <u>These</u> like to sail, hike, and climb mountains.
               D

Unit 4

Possessive Adjectives

Exercise 1.   **Realia** Complete this conversation by writing the correct possessive adjective (*my, your, his, her, its, our, their*) in each blank.

John: Look at this picture. Yuki looks like you.

Mary: No, ❶ _____ hair is short and ❷ _____ hair is long.

John: Yes, but both of ❸ _____ dresses have stripes. Does Makoto look like me?

Mary: No! ❹ _____ hair is straight. ❺ _____ hair is curly.

John: Well, they have a pet, and so do we!

Mary: Yes, but ❻ _____ pet is a cat. ❼ _____ pet is a bird!

John: OK. But ❽ _____ name is Tori, which is Japanese for "bird"!!!

Mary: Oh, really? That's strange.

Exercise 2. **Original Sentence Writing** Write true sentences to describe your family, friends, and pets. Use possessive adjectives (*my, his, her, your, our, its, their*). Study the examples.

examples: my friend   His eyes are brown.

        my aunt   Her house is really big.

1. me   _____

2. my mother   _____

3. my father   _____

4. my brother(s)   _____

5. my sister(s)   _____

6. my grandparents   _____

7. my teacher   _____

8. my dentist   _____

9. my doctor   _____

10. my pet   _____

Exercise 3. **Realia** Fill in the blanks with the correct possessive adjectives and the matching automobile features.

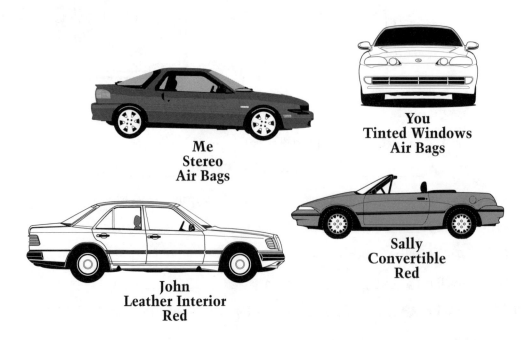

Me
Stereo
Air Bags

You
Tinted Windows
Air Bags

John
Leather Interior
Red

Sally
Convertible
Red

1. I love music. _____ car has a _____ .

2. John likes luxury. _____ car has a _____ .

3. Sally likes the wind in her face. _____ car is a _____ .

4. We think safety is important. _____ cars must have _____ .

5. John and Sally like red. _____ cars are _____ .

6. Since the sun is so bright, _____ car has _____ .

7. One car is luxurious. _____ interior is _____ .

Exercise 4.   **Puzzle/Game** This puzzle has three steps. In step 1, write the correct possessive adjective on the lines in the sentences. Next, look at the Secret Code in the box below. Find the secret letter that corresponds to each of your answers in step 1. Finally, write that letter in the line above the numbers in the Riddle Box. For example, if your answer for number 3 is *your,* then you should write the letter *e* in the blank for number 3. (This one has been done for you.) If your answers are correct, you can answer the riddle below.

Step 1.   1. I have my pen, and she has _____ pen.

2. My brother and I have a new apartment. Do you know _____ new address?

3. "Sue, how many TVs does __your__ family have?"

4. Ann, Paul, and I did well on _____ final exams.

5. Tourists have to show _____ passports when they enter a new country.

6. Where do you buy _____ shirts? They always look so nice.

7. I can't find _____ keys.

8. Poor cat! _____ tail is hurt.

9. Mr. Smith drives _____ car to the office every day except Friday.

10. Do you, Kenny, and Paul have _____ IDs with you?

Step 2.

THE SECRET CODE				
he = R	her = A	your = E	its = O	my = L
she = B	our = N	his = P	they = T	their = V

Step 3. Riddle: What starts with "e," ends with "e," and has one letter in it?

ANSWER: __ __ *e* __ __ __ __ __ __ __
         1 2   3 4 5 6 7 8 9 10

Exercise 5. **Dialogue and Conversation Practice** Dave and Mark are talking about classes. Write a dialogue that includes teachers' names, class size, titles of books, other students' names, and anything else you want. Be sure to use possessive adjectives.

Dave: Hi, Mark. Where is your grammar class?

Mark: It's in Cooper Hall.

Dave: _____

Mark: _____

Dave: _____

Mark: _____

Dave: _____

Mark: _____

Dave: _____

Mark: _____

Exercise 6. **Sentence Study** Read the beginning sentences. Then read the answer choices and put a check mark in front of **all of the sentences that are true** based on the beginning sentences. Remember that more than one answer is possible sometimes.

1. My uncle Carl is my mother's brother.
   ___ a. My brother is my uncle.
   ___ b. I have a brother named Carl.
   ___ c. My mother has a brother.
   ___ d. I have an uncle named Carl.

2. Our teacher has a parrot. Its name is Pollie.
   ___ a. Our teacher is a parrot.
   ___ b. The bird belongs to the teacher.
   ___ c. Our teacher's name is Mrs. Pollie.
   ___ d. Pollie is the name of our teacher's parrot.

3. Laura and I went to the mall yesterday, and she bought a blue dress.
   ___ a. My new dress is blue.
   ___ b. I bought a new dress for Laura.
   ___ c. Her new dress is blue.
   ___ d. Laura bought her dress at the mall.

4. My husband and I went out to dinner and a movie last night.
   ___ a. We saw a movie last night.
   ___ b. We ate dinner in a restaurant last night.
   ___ c. My husband went to dinner, and I went to a movie.
   ___ d. We didn't like our dinner.

5. *Teacher:* "Please close your books and take out a piece of paper."
   ___ a. The students are not permitted to use their books.
   ___ b. The students are permitted to use the books.
   ___ c. The students can use paper, but they cannot use the books.
   ___ d. The students are looking for their books and papers.

6. *Kelly:* "Can you help me find my glasses? I can't see."
   ___ a. Kelly lost her glasses.
   ___ b. Kelly lost my glasses.
   ___ c. Kelly found your glasses.
   ___ d. Kelly can't see without her glasses.

7. *Linda:* "My three brothers go to the university. My only sister is in high school."
   ___ a. Her parents have five children.
   ___ b. His brothers attend the university.
   ___ c. Her sister is not in the university.
   ___ d. Her brothers attend the university.

8. Sarah is a student at Miami City College. She attends school only in the morning. She has a grammar class at 9:00 A.M., history class at 10:00 A.M., and literature class at 11:00 A.M.
   ___ a. Her classes are in the morning.
   ___ b. Her college is in Miami.
   ___ c. Her history class is at 9:00.
   ___ d. She has three classes.

Exercise 7. **TOEFL Review**

Part 1. Completion. For items 1 through 8, circle the letter of the answer that best completes the statement or question.

1. I have a new horse! __ name is Misty.

    a. It's

    b. Its

    c. My

    d. She

2. May I borrow __ eraser? I don't have one.

    a. your

    b. my

    c. you're

    d. yours

3. An American woman sometimes takes __ husband's last name.

    a. her

    b. his

    c. she

    d. him

4. __ rich uncle flies his helicopter to visit me.

    a. I

    b. My

    c. Me

    d. He

5. We like Mrs. Norman. She is __ favorite teacher.

    a. their

    b. her

    c. we

    d. our

6. "Can you pick us up at the airport tomorrow?"

"Yes, what time does ___ flight arrive?"

a. your

b. my

c. our

d. their

7. My grandparents live in Florida. ___ house is near the beach.

a. My

b. Their

c. It's

d. They're

8. That is my mother's favorite chair. Please don't sit in ___ chair.

a. its

b. hers

c. your

d. her

Part 2. Error Identification. For items 9 through 15, read each sentence carefully. Look at the underlined parts. Circle the letter that shows the incorrect part.

9. We have many books at <u>our house</u>. Some are <u>my books</u>, but most belong to <u>my</u>
                       A   B   C

brother. <u>He</u> books are expensive.
        D

10. *A:* "The sky looks cloudy today. I have some advice for you."

   B: "What's that?"

   A: "<u>I advice</u> is to take <u>your umbrella</u>."
         A   B

   B: "Thanks. I think I will take <u>my coat</u> and <u>boots</u>, too."
                                   C   D

11. These are <u>my car keys</u>. <u>You car keys</u> are on the table. <u>My keys</u> don't work in <u>your car</u>.
                A   B   C   D

12. <u>My favorite colors</u> are pink and green, but Linda likes blue and white. <u>Our living room</u>
       A   B

is decorated in one of <u>her favorite colors</u> and one of <u>we favorite colors</u>. It is
                   C   D

beautifully decorated in green and blue!

13. <u>My grandmother</u> has a new cat. <u>It's name</u> is Lily. <u>It is</u> a Himalayn cat. When I visit
     A   B   C

her, the cat sits on <u>my lap</u>.
                   D

14. "<u>Do you like</u> songs by Janet Jackson? She is <u>my favorite</u> music artist." "No, I don't
       A   B

like <u>she music</u>. I prefer Celine Dion. <u>Her voice</u> is beautiful."
     C   D

15. I have a noise problem with <u>her neighbors</u>. <u>They're</u> very noisy. <u>They have</u> parties,
                              A   B   C

and <u>their TV</u> is too loud. I need to move to a new apartment.
     D

Unit 5

Past Tense of *Be*

Exercise 1. **Realia** Two people are discussing photos in a photo album. Read their dialogue and underline the correct forms of the verb *be.*

Teresa: Jill, who is this person?

Jill: That's my younger sister. Her name is Sarah.

Teresa: I see in this picture that she ❶ (is, was) on the softball team in high school.

Jill: Yes, that's correct. She ❷ (were, was) a great player.

Teresa: How did you and your sister get along?

Jill: Great. We ❸ (are, were) always together when we were kids . . . going to school, playing in the park, just about everything.

Teresa: What about now? ❹ (Are, Were) you close to your sister?

Jill: Not so much. The problem is that we ❺ (aren't, weren't) near each other anymore.

Teresa: So you don't see her so much?

Jill: No, she lives in Seattle. She ❻ (is, was) here in Florida two years ago on vacation.

Teresa: Do you talk to her on the phone?

Jill: Not so often. Last week I **7** (is, was) in Washington State on a business trip, and I called her.

Teresa: And . . . ?

Jill: She and her husband **8** (are, were) out of town the day I called.

Teresa: I have the same problem with some of my family members, too. It's a shame that we live so far apart.

Exercise 2.   **Original Sentence Writing** Read the following words and write sentences using those words. Use the correct verb tense and form.

1. My best subject in high school . . .

   _____

2. My worst subject in high school . . .

   _____

3. The happiest event in my life . . .

   _____

   _____

4. The most expensive thing I ever bought . . .

   _____

5. The three most important people in the twentieth century . . .

   _____

   _____

6. The three most important inventions in the twentieth century . . .

   _____

   _____

Exercise 3. **Realia** Read the following e-mail message from Amina to her brother Djaouad. Write the correct form of the verb *be* in the spaces. Sometimes you will have to use a negative form.

```
Date: Mon. 2 Aug. 1999 12:09:45     -0400 (EDT)
From: amd@intl.com
To:  djd@lifenet.com
Subject: ARE YOU OKAY???


Dear Djaouad,

Where ❶_____ you last night???  I tried and tried to call you,
but you ❷_____ home.  Please write me back soon so that I know
that you ❸_____ okay now.

Here ❹_____ some news from home.  Mom ❺_____ sick
last week, so Dad and I took her to the doctor.  We ❻_____
at the office for 4 hours.  She's okay, but I think she misses you very
much.  You live so far away, and she loves you so much.  Please call
her soon, okay?

So, how are your classes? ❼_____ you busy with schoolwork?
How ❽_____ your test  last week?  Did you get a good grade?

Write me back soon and remember to call Mom.

I love you,

Amina
From: amd@intl.com
```

Exercise 4.   **Puzzle/Game**   Read the clues for the crossword puzzle. Underline the correct verb forms and fill in the blanks. Then fill in the answers in the puzzle.

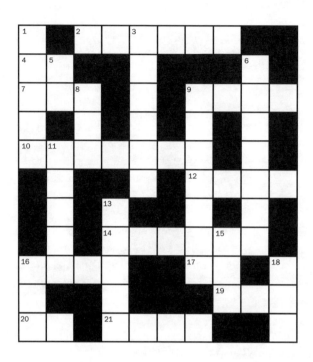

Across

2. This country (*was, is*) the World Cup Champion in 1998. _____

4. The best way _____ go from here to Europe (*is, are*) by plane. Travel by ship takes too long!

7. If you subtract thirty-nine from forty, the answer (*is, are*) _____ .

9. If you (*are, is*) at the beach too long, your skin will _____ .

10. This famous singer (*was, were*) married to Sean Penn. _____

12. The news about the death of the president (*was, were*) not false. It (*was, were*) _____ .

Down

1. There (*was, were*) a big _____ last night. The wind and rain were so bad!

3. This city (*is, was*) the capital of Greece. _____

5. I visit China many times because of my business. My last trip to China (*are, was*) _____ June 21.

6. This small country (*is, was*) in the southern part of South America. _____

8. The _____ of the twentieth century (*was, were*) December 31, 1999.

Across

14. We (*was, were*) _____ in class yesterday because we studied until 5 A.M.

16. The meaning of the word *speak* (*is, was*) similar to the meaning of the word _____ .

17. Did you taste the cake that Kerry made? That cake (*was, were*) _____ delicious!

19. If you multiply five times two, the answer (*is, was*) _____ .

20. I asked Jim if he wanted to go to the movie with us, but his answer (*is, was*) _____ because he wanted to watch TV instead.

21. He (*was, were*) a famous Spanish painter whose first name was Salvador. _____

Down

9. This (*was, were*) a famous singing group from Great Britain. _____

11. What (*is, are*) the name of the girl in the e-mail in the previous exercise? _____

13. Yesterday's grammar class (*was, is*) so difficult. I _____ the teacher to explain it again.

15. When I go to Mark's house, there (*is, are*) always a _____ of food cooking on the stove.

16. What (*is, are*) the answer to number 19 across? _____

18. The number of thumbs on one hand (*is, are*) _____ .

───

Exercise 5. **Dialogue and Conversation Practice** Ralph and Dimitri are friends. Ralph is worried about Dimitri because yesterday he seemed sad. Write a dialogue (questions and answers) using at least six of the vocabulary words below.

sad	worried	angry	upset	tired
yesterday	home	last night	test	called

Ralph: _____

Dimitri: _____

Ralph: _____

Dimitri: _____

Ralph: _____

Dimitri: _____

Ralph: _____

Dimitri: _____

Ralph: _____

Dimitri: _____

Exercise 6.   **Sentence Study** Read the beginning sentences. Then read the answer choices and put a check mark in front of **all of the sentences that are true** based on the beginning sentences. Remember that more than one answer is possible sometimes.

1. The steaks and the cake were delicious, and the broccoli salad was excellent.
   ___ a. There was broccoli in the salad.
   ___ b. There was lettuce in the salad.
   ___ c. The food was very good.
   ___ d. The cake was very good.

2. *Keith:* "How was your picnic on Sunday?"
   Elena: "We had a good time. Diane and a few other friends went with me."
   Keith: "The weather was really good on Sunday."
   Elena: "Yes, it was perfect for an afternoon picnic."
   ___ a. Only two people were at the picnic.
   ___ b. Only three people were at the picnic.
   ___ c. More than three people were at the picnic.
   ___ d. The weather on Sunday afternoon was great.

3. Work begins at 9 A.M. All of the office workers were on time except for Nathan.
   ___ a. Nathan arrived after 9 A.M.
   ___ b. The other workers arrived at the office before Nathan.
   ___ c. Nathan was late for work.
   ___ d. Only one person was late.

4. The restaurant was empty last night.
   ___ a. There were a lot of people at the restaurant.
   ___ b. There weren't a lot of people at the restaurant.
   ___ c. There were a lot of waiters in the restaurant.
   ___ d. The food in the restaurant is sometimes expensive.

5. My friends weren't happy with their test scores.
   ___ a. Their grades were good.
   ___ b. They didn't receive grades.
   ___ c. Their grades were not so good.
   ___ d. They don't want to make the same grades on the next test.

6. My car wasn't in the garage during the rainstorm.
   ___ a. Now my car is wet.
   ___ b. Now my car is very hot.
   ___ c. Now my car is not working well.
   ___ d. Now my car is far from the garage.

7. *Bob:*   "How was your flight? Did you have a good seat?"
   Jim: "My seat was 21-A. I was next to the window."
   Lynn: "My seat was 21-C. I was sitting next to the aisle."
   ___ a. Jim and Bob were on a plane.
   ___ b. Lynn and Bob were on a plane.
   ___ c. Jim and Lynn were on a plane.
   ___ d. Bob, Jim, and Lynn were on a plane.

8. Leslie was the winner of the bowling tournament.
   ___ a. Leslie was happy about this.
   ___ b. Leslie was sad about this.
   ___ c. Leslie was angry about this.
   ___ d. Leslie was sick after this happened.

Exercise 7.   **TOEFL Review**

Part 1.   Completion. For items 1 through 8, circle the letter of the answer that best completes the statement or question.

1. Why ___ you absent yesterday?

   a. were

   b. are

   c. be

   d. aren't

2. Was the book interesting?

   No, it ___ .

   a. was

   b. isn't

   c. weren't

   d. wasn't

3. Harry ___ at Daniel's house last night.

   a. was

   b. is

   c. is not

   d. no was

4. How were your final exams?

   They ___ so easy!

   a. are

   b. were

   c. was

   d. be

5. Was the librarian helpful?

   Yes, ___ .

   a. she did

   b. she wasn't

   c. she was

   d. was she

6. Where ___ born?

   a. were you

   b. you

   c. did you

   d. is you

7. My mother and father ___ angry with me yesterday.

   a. was

   b. is

   c. were

   d. they

8. My book bag ___ stolen from my locker this morning!

   a. is

   b. was

   c. not

   d. am

Part 2. Error Identification. For items 9 through 15, read each sentence carefully. Look at the underlined parts. Circle the letter that shows the incorrect part of the sentence.

9. <u>Last</u> night's <u>classical music</u> concert <u>were</u> very <u>good</u>.
     A   B   C   D

10. <u>Is</u> yesterday's <u>grammar</u> class <u>interesting</u> or <u>boring</u>?
     A   B   C   D

11. The <u>students were</u> excited when <u>their</u> got <u>good</u> grades on <u>the test</u>.
             A   B   C   D

12. <u>Yesterday's</u> <u>cafeteria</u> <u>dinner</u> <u>not</u> good.
       A   B   C   D

13. <u>Were</u> Barbara's <u>graduation</u> party <u>last night</u> <u>fun</u>?
      A   B   C   D

14. <u>Was</u> you born <u>in</u> Los Angeles <u>or</u> New York <u>City</u>?
     A   B   C   D

15. <u>You</u> with <u>your</u> family <u>or</u> your <u>friends</u> yesterday?
     A   B   C   D

Unit 6

Past Tense of Regular and Irregular Verbs

Exercise 1. **Realia** Read the postcard from Yoko to her new friend, Jorge, in Spain. Fill in each blank with the correct form of the verb in parentheses.

Dear Jorge,

Hi. How are you? I am fine. I am having a wonderful time here in Florida. This morning, my brother and I sat on the beach and (watch) ❶ _____ the sunrise and (listen) ❷ _____ to the ocean. I brought my guitar and (play) ❸ _____ it for a while. It was very beautiful. My brother spent the day at the beach. He (learn) ❹ _____ how to surf in only a few hours! I really (want) ❺ _____ to do it, so he (try) ❻ _____ to teach me. I (understand, neg) ❼ _____ his instructions, so he (explain) ❽ _____ them to me again, and I (practice) ❾ _____ all day. Be sure to write to me soon!

Love,
Yoko

Mr. Jorge Santander

2517 La Siena Way

Los Angeles, CA

70741

Exercise 2.   **Original Sentence Writing** Read the following words and write sentences using those words. You may have to change some word forms. Write affirmative statements, negative statements, and questions in the past tense. Add capital letters as needed. Pay attention to the punctuation at the ends of the blanks to help you decide if you should write a statement or a question.

1. watch / Nora / tennis / on television

   _____ .

2. do / Kurt / his homework / (neg)

   _____ .

3. mail / you / the letter

   _____ ?

4. eat / Jennifer / the lasagna

   _____ .

5. like / Elias / the fish / (neg)

   _____ .

6. rain / it / last night

   _____ ?

7. hear / the dog / a noise outside

   _____ .

8. sleep / I / last night / (neg)

   _____ .

9. understand / you / the teacher

   _____ ?

10. go / we / to the beach / yesterday

    _____ .

11. buy / Tyler / vegetables

    _____ .

12. read / you / this book

    _____ ?

Exercise 3.   **Realia** Read the letter a student wrote to her local newspaper columnist named "Mr. Advice." In her letter, the student asked for help with a problem. After you read the letter, read the response that follows. Fill in each blank with the correct form of the verb in parentheses.

Dear Mr. Advice:

I need your help! I am a college student with a very difficult roommate. Let me tell you my problem. Two weeks ago, my roommate **1** (begin) _____ guitar lessons. Unfortunately, she **2** (practice) _____every night, and she **3** (do)_____ it in our room! **4** (think) _____ she _____ about me? No, she didn't. **5** (play) _____ she _____ quietly? No, she didn't. She **6** (think, neg) _____ about me at all! I **7** (go) _____ to the store and **8** (buy) _____ some ear plugs, but that **9** (help, neg) _____, so I **10** (speak) _____ to her and she **11** (tell) _____ me to put the pillow over my head!

Please, Mr. Advice, help me!

Sincerely,

Sleepless in Sarasota

Dear Sleepless:

It seems that you **12** (give) _____ your roommate many chances to change and she didn't. Wish her luck with her guitar lessons and find another roommate!

Mr. Advice

Exercise 4.   **Puzzle/Game**   Read the clues for the crossword puzzle. Fill in the blanks. Then fill in the answers in the puzzle.

Across

1. past tense of *bring* _____

4. past tense of *choose* _____

6. simple form of *was* and *were*

_____

7. past tense of *give* _____

9. past tense of *make* _____

11. past tense of *speak* _____

12. past tense of *go* _____

16. past tense of *understand*

_____

18. past tense of *eat* _____

20. past tense of *think* _____

22. present tense of *went* _____

23. past tense of *drink* _____

Down

1. past tense of *begin* _____

2. present tense of *used* _____

3. past tense of *hide* _____

4. past tense of *come* _____

5. present tense of *saw* _____

8. past tense of *vote* _____

10. past tense of *do* _____

11. past tense of *stand* _____

13. past tense of *sleep* _____

14. past tense of *put* _____

15. past tense of *hear* _____

17. past tense of *take* _____

19. present tense of *did* _____

21. present tense of *went* _____

Exercise 5.   **Dialogue and Conversation Practice** Roberto is talking to his friend Linda about what he did over the weekend. Complete the dialogue below. Use the past tense of the verbs in parentheses to help you.

Linda: Hi, Roberto! How are you?

Roberto: I am tired. I had a very busy weekend.

Linda: Really? What did you do this weekend?

Roberto: (go / a store)

    1. _____

    _____ .

Linda: Did you buy anything?

Roberto: (buy / shirt)

    2. _____

    _____ .

Linda: Which shirt did you choose?

Roberto: (choose / blue shirt)

    3. _____

    _____ .

Linda: That sounds good. What did you do on Saturday?

Roberto: (make / cake)

    4. _____ .

Linda: How did you make the cake?

Roberto: (read / the directions)

    5. _____ .

Linda: Oh! I wanted to ask you. Did you see your parents on Saturday?

Roberto: (see / my parents)

    6. _____ .

Linda: That's great! I'm sure you were happy to see them. What did you do on Sunday?

Roberto: (my friends / come over)

    7. _____ and

    (we / eat lunch)

    8. _____ .

Linda: That sounds wonderful! Did you speak English with your friends?

Roberto: (speak / English)

    9. _____ .

Linda: It sounds like you had a great weekend. Good for you!

Exercise 6. **Sentence Study** Read the beginning sentences. Then read the answer choices and put a check mark in front of **all of the sentences that are true** based on the beginning sentences. Remember that more than one answer is possible sometimes.

1. Linda spoke to the people at the party. She didn't understand everything they said, but she didn't want to ask them to repeat it.
   ___ a. Linda didn't speak at the party.
   ___ b. Linda asked people to repeat what they said.
   ___ c. Linda understood what everyone said.
   ___ d. Linda didn't ask people to repeat what they said.

2. Don asked Nina for help with his homework because it was difficult. She didn't understand it either.
   ___ a. Don understood his homework.
   ___ b. Nina didn't understand Don's homework.
   ___ c. Nina understood Don's homework.
   ___ d. Don didn't ask Nina for help.

3. Nancy didn't like the purple shirts, so she chose the red shirts instead. She bought two red shirts.
   ___ a. Nancy didn't buy red shirts.
   ___ b. Nancy didn't buy purple shirts.
   ___ c. Nancy bought red shirts.
   ___ d. Nancy didn't like the purple shirts.

4. Seymour ate a whole pizza and drank three glasses of soda. He was sick for two days.
   ___ a. Seymour was on a special diet.
   ___ b. Only Seymour ate the pizza.
   ___ c. Seymour didn't feel well for two days.
   ___ d. Seymour is not happy that he ate the pizza.

5. Louise didn't feel well yesterday, so she visited the doctor. The doctor said she is healthy.
   ___ a. Louise didn't see the doctor.
   ___ b. The doctor saw Louise.
   ___ c. The doctor says that Louise is not sick.
   ___ d. Louise felt sick.

6. Sheila and Takako went to a club and danced for hours. Then, they went home and listened to music.
   ___ a. Sheila and Takako like to listen to music.
   ___ b. Sheila and Takako are listening to music now.
   ___ c. Sheila and Takako didn't dance in the club.
   ___ d. Sheila and Takako were at the club for hours.

7. Chris came to my party and met many people. She saw an old friend and talked for hours with him about old times.
   __ a. Chris saw an old friend.
   __ b. The old friend was a man.
   __ c. Chris went to a party.
   __ d. Chris talked to many people on the phone.

8. Fred flew to Los Angeles and spent the week with his sister. They drove around the city and saw many interesting sights.
   __ a. Fred visited his sister.
   __ b. Fred's sister saw many interesting sights.
   __ c. Fred was alone in Los Angeles.
   __ d. Fred lives in Los Angeles.

Exercise 7.   **TOEFL Review**

Part 1.   Completion. For items 1 through 8, circle the letter of the answer that best completes the statement or question.

1. Paula __ for her test, so she failed it.

   a. not study

   b. no study

   c. didn't study

   d. didn't studied

2. __ Bertha __ to school, or did she drive her car?

   a. Did . . . walked

   b. Did . . . walk

   c. Did . . . walks

   d. Did . . . walking

3. The police officer __ that car because the driver was speeding.

   a. stopped

   b. stopping

   c. stoped

   d. stops

4. Fred ___ his car last night.

   a. was washed

   b. washed

   c. were washed

   d. washing

5. Maria ___ to understand her teacher.

   a. tryed

   b. was tryed

   c. tried

   d. was tried

6. Louise ___ the spaghetti for very long.

   a. didn't cooked

   b. didn't cook

   c. no cook

   d. not cooked

7. Anthony ___ to care for his grass, so he paid someone to do it.

   a. no liked

   b. not liked

   c. didn't like

   d. liked not

8. Terry and Bob ___ on the weekend.

   a. didn't study

   b. no studied

   c. studied not

   d. doesn't studied

Part 2. Error Identification. For items 9 through 15, read each sentence carefully. Look at the underlined parts. Circle the letter that shows the incorrect part.

9. My mother and I <u>watched</u> television last night. We <u>were surprised</u> when we <u>seed</u> that
                 A   B   C

    the forecast <u>was</u> bad.
                  D

10. Fred <u>wanted</u> to wash his car, but he <u>know</u> that the weather <u>was</u> bad, so he <u>didn't do</u> it.
         A   B   C   D

11. Ellen and Benjamin <u>didn't played</u> outside because their mother <u>told</u> them to <u>come</u>
                         A   B   C

    inside and <u>eat</u> dinner.
             D

12. Nancy <u>asked</u> her teacher for help because she <u>didn't understood</u> the lesson, so the
            A   B

    teacher <u>helped</u> her <u>do</u> her homework.
            C   D

13. My mother <u>was angry</u> when my brother <u>standed</u> outside in the rain. She <u>didn't want</u>
               A   B   C

    him to <u>get</u> sick.
        D

14. Barry <u>didn't eat</u> much food for several weeks, and he <u>lost</u> a lot of weight. He <u>tried</u> to
        A   B   C

    exercise also, but he <u>no had</u> time.
                 D

15. Jim <u>no was</u> available to help anyone with the work, so many people <u>had</u> problems
       A   B

    <u>completing</u> their jobs. People prefer to have Jim around when <u>they're working</u>.
      C   D

Unit 7

Wh- Questions

Exercise 1. **Realia** Look at the following advertisement for a travel agency. Fill in the missing question words.

Hello Travelers!

Do you ever ask yourself these questions???

_____ country do you want to visit?   Italy? Japan? Brazil?

_____ do you want to see?   Old monuments? Nature? Folk dancing?

_____ do you like to travel?   In the summer? In the spring?

_____ do you like to travel with?   Friends? Family?

No matter what type of vacation you prefer, 123 TRAVEL can help you find the perfect vacation!

Call us now. We have a friendly and professional team of travel agents who can help you.

1-800-111-1111
or e-mail us at: 123travel@comnet.com
123 TRAVEL . . . we are at your service!

Exercise 2.   **Original Sentence Writing** Read the following sentences that answer a question. In the blanks, write a question using *what, when, where, why, who,* or *which.* (Note: *whom* is possible, also. If you have studied *whom,* you may use it.)

1. _____

I want <u>the red pen, not the blue one.</u>

2. _____

They went <u>to Ecuador.</u>

3. _____

I went home <u>because I was sleepy.</u>

4. _____

Lisa went to the park with <u>Raoul.</u>

5. _____

I ate <u>pancakes</u> for breakfast.

6. _____

Shelly got home <u>at 10 P.M.</u>

7. _____

The students did poorly on the test <u>because they didn't study.</u>

8. _____

My sister and I were <u>at the library</u> last night.

──────

Exercise 3.   **Realia** A police detective is questioning someone who recently saw a crime. Read the following report and fill in the missing *wh-* words.

Detective:	❶_____ were you doing on Elm Street last night, Mr. Jones?
Mr. Jones:	I was walking my dog.
Detective:	And ❷_____ were you at exactly 8 P.M.?
Mr. Jones:	I was in front of the drugstore.
Detective:	❸_____ did you go to the drugstore?
Mr. Jones:	I had a headache, so I wanted to buy some aspirin.
Detective:	❹_____ did you see walk into the store?
Mr. Jones:	I saw a tall blond man enter the store. He was about 25 years old.
Detective:	❺_____ clothes did he have on?
Mr. Jones:	He had blue jeans and a white T-shirt. And tennis shoes, I think.
Detective:	❻_____ did the man go in the store?
Mr. Jones:	He went directly to the cashier.
Detective:	❼_____ did he do at that time?
Mr. Jones:	I heard him ask the cashier for all the money. That's when I took out my cellular phone and called the police.
Detective:	❽_____ were you standing when you made the phone call?
Mr. Jones:	I was standing next to the soda machine. The man didn't see me.
Detective:	Thank you very much for your help. We will call you if we need extra information.

Exercise 4. **Puzzle/Game** Read the following answers to popular trivia questions. Then use the question words (*What, When, Where, Why, Who, Which*) in the box on the left and the nouns in the box on the right to make questions. Write the questions in the blanks. Use the underlined parts as clues for the correct questions to ask.

| What When Where Why Who Which | **+** | the Coliseum the Taj Mahal the Great Pyramids the Berlin Wall Princess Diana e-mail Neil Armstrong the Panama Canal | **=** | _____ **?** |

1. __What is the Taj Mahal?_____

   It is a beautiful white <u>building</u> in India.

2. _____

   This large monument is in <u>Rome, Italy</u>.

3. _____

   It is important <u>because ships need to travel more quickly between the Atlantic and</u>

   <u>Pacific Oceans</u>.

4. _____

   They are located in <u>Giza, Egypt</u>.

5. _____

   The German people took it down <u>in 1989</u>.

6. _____

   He was <u>the first man to walk on the moon</u>.

7. _____

   It means "<u>electronic mail</u>."

8. _____

   She died in a tragic car accident <u>in 1997</u>.

Exercise 5. **Dialogue and Conversation Practice** June and Marilyn are friends. June wants to know what Marilyn did over the weekend. Write a dialogue (questions and answers) using at least four of the vocabulary words below.

| Where | Why | When | What | Who | Which |

June: _____

_____

Marilyn: _____

_____

June: _____

_____

Marilyn: _____

_____

June: _____

_____

Marilyn: _____

_____

June: _____

_____

Marilyn: _____

_____

Exercise 6. **Sentence Study** The sentences below each begin with a question word (*when, where, which,* etc.). Read the beginning sentences. Then read the answer choices and put a check mark in front of **all of the answers that are possible** based on the question words in the question. Remember that more than one answer is possible sometimes.

1. When did Michael come to the United States?
   ___ a. For a year.
   ___ b. In 1997.
   ___ c. Next year.
   ___ d. A few years ago.

2. What did he study in his first year in college?
   ___ a. Economics.
   ___ b. With his best friend.
   ___ c. International business.
   ___ d. Basic writing skills.

3. Where did the boys go last weekend?
   ___ a. Because they had a vacation.
   ___ b. To the zoo.
   ___ c. At approximately 8:00 P.M.
   ___ d. To the mall north of town.

4. Which movie did you see?
   ___ a. In the mall.
   ___ b. The comedy.
   ___ c. Three times.
   ___ d. With several of my closest friends.

5. Where did Susan go?
   ___ a. To the airport.
   ___ b. To a meeting.
   ___ c. From her house.
   ___ d. From noon to midnight.

6. When did you get home?
   ___ a. The stores closed.
   ___ b. Because it rained.
   ___ c. After dark.
   ___ d. A little after seven.

7. Why did you come to class late?
   ___ a. My alarm clock was broken.
   ___ b. By bike.
   ___ c. It was October.
   ___ d. I am not a morning person, so it's hard for me to get up on time.

8. Which exercise did we do in the last class?
   ___ a. The exercise about question words.
   ___ b. In the back of the book.
   ___ c. The one on page 37.
   ___ d. It was very easy.

Exercise 7.

Part 1. Completion. For items 1 through 8, circle the letter of the answer that best completes the question.

1. ___ the man tired?

   a. Why is

   b. Why

   c. Are

   d. Did

2. ___ you do yesterday?

   a. What do

   b. Why did

   c. What did

   d. Where did

3. ___ the dictionary?

   a. Where are

   b. Where

   c. Why is

   d. Where is

4. Excuse me. Where ___?

   a. the library is

   b. the library

   c. is the library

   d. are the library

5. When ___?

   a. does the bus leaves

   b. leaves the bus

   c. does the bus leave

   d. bus leaves

6. ___ born?

    a. Where was you

    b. Where you

    c. Where you were

    d. Where were you

7. We have two types of cookies. ___ do you prefer?

    a. Which type

    b. Where type

    c. Type which

    d. Why type

8. ___ the swimming pool closed?

    a. Where is

    b. Does

    c. Are

    d. Why is

Part 2. Error Identification. For items 9 through 15, read each sentence carefully. Look at the underlined parts. Circle the letter that shows the incorrect part of the sentence.

9. <u>Why</u> does Billy do <u>every day</u> <u>after</u> <u>school</u>?
   A   B   C   D

10. <u>Why</u> <u>was</u> you and Lucy so <u>sad</u> <u>yesterday?</u>
   A   B   C   D

11. <u>When</u> <u>were</u> you <u>come home</u> from work <u>last night</u>?
   A   B   C   D

12. Pardon <u>me</u>. <u>When</u> time <u>does</u> the bus usually <u>arrive</u>?
             A   B   C   D

13. <u>Why</u> did <u>they</u> <u>ate</u> all the <u>cake</u>?
   A   B   C   D

14. <u>Who</u> <u>are</u> your <u>favorite</u> teacher at <u>this</u> school?
   A   B   C   D

15. <u>Who</u> <u>study</u> algebra <u>with</u> Mr. Rogers <u>the year before last</u>?
   A   B   C   D

Unit 8

Word Order

Exercise 1. **Realia** Your friend Celia is a busy woman. She left her calendar at your house. She calls you on the telephone and wants you to read her schedule to her. Answer the following questions that she asks you. Use complete sentences.

Monday	12:00	dentist	
Tuesday	9:30	breakfast with Sally	Country Inn
Tuesday	3:30	take Jane to dance class	Steptoe Academy
Wednesday	11:00	meet realtor	1432 E. Branson St.
Wednesday	3:00	apply for loan	Union Bank
Thursday	11:30	lunch with Patricia Cole	London Tea Room
Friday	7:00	movie with Paul	

1. When do I go to the dentist?

   _____

2. What do I do Tuesday morning?

   _____

3. When is Jane's dance class?

   _____

4. What happens on Wednesday morning?

   _____

5. What about Wednesday afternoon?

   _____

6. Do I have a lunch meeting this week? With whom? Where?

_____

7. This week looks really busy. I'm going to be so tired at the end of the week. Am I

doing anything for fun? When?

_____

Exercise 2.   **Original Sentence Writing** Read the following words and write
sentences using those words. You may have to change some word
forms. Add capital letters as needed. Be sure to add a period at the
end of each statement and a question mark at the end of each
question.

example: on Friday / does he have / at noon / class
          Does he have class at noon on Friday? _____

1. on Sunday mornings / at home / I / eat / a hot breakfast

_____

2. I / at 7:00 A.M. / get up / on Monday, Tuesday, and Wednesday

_____

3. do you / to the beach / go / in the summer

_____

4. in room 205 / Mrs. Gridley was / last night / at General Hospital

_____

5. my cousin / in the morning / likes to run

_____

6. at the University of Florida / he / in his dormitory room / have / a computer / does

_____

7. every Saturday / breakfast / like to eat / on Fourth Street / Laura and Larry / at the

Eggery

_____

8. works / during the summer / on a cruise ship / Paul / in the Caribbean

_____

Exercise 3.   **Realia**   Underline the correct words to complete this advertisement for Alaska. Pay attention to the form of the adjective and the word order.

Visit the Great Land
ALASKA

- Play all day and night in the Land of the ❶ (Midnight Sun, Sun Midnight)
- Touch ❷ (ancient glaciers, glaciers ancient, ancients glaciers)
- Take photos of ❸ (bears brown mighty, mighty brown bears, mighty browns bears)
- Climb the ❹ (majestics mountains, mountains majestic, majestic mountains)
- View the ❺ (tallest mountain, mountain tallest) in North America
- Learn the history of the ❻ (adventurous gold miners, gold miners adventurous)
- Go fishing for ❼ (famous Alaskan salmon, salmon Alaskan famous)
- Cruise the ocean and watch for ❽ (whales gray, gray whales, grays whales)

Exercise 4.   **Puzzle/Game**   Use the adjective list on the right to fill in the blanks for the clues. Then fill in the answers in the puzzle.

Adjectives

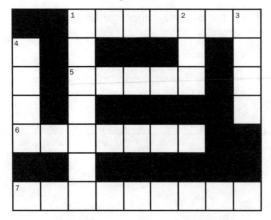

deep	natural
sour	nervous
delicious	odd
tired	perfect

Across:

1. He is _____ about the test.

5. I feel very _____ after I play

   soccer.

6. A _____ exam means you

   didn't make any mistakes.

7. My grandmother makes

   _____ pies.

Down

1. I prefer _____ spring water.

2. 1, 3, 5, and 7 are _____

   numbers.

3. Lemons are _____ .

4. The ocean is very _____ .

Exercise 5.   **Dialogue and Conversation Practice** Mary works in a department store. She is the manager of the boys' department. She has new shirts to sell. There are blue shirts, green shirts, and yellow shirts. She wants a different size on each shelf (top, middle, bottom).

Lorraine is helping Mary, but Lorraine doesn't know where to put the shirts. Write a dialogue between Mary and Lorraine in which Lorraine asks Mary how to arrange the shirts.

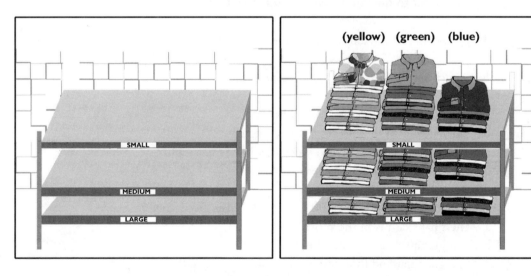

Mary: Here are the new shirts that I ordered. Look! There are three really beautiful colors.

Lorraine: _____

Mary: _____

Lorraine: _____

Mary: _____

Lorraine: _____

Mary: _____

Lorraine: _____

Mary: _____

Lorraine: _____

Exercise 6. **Sentence Study** Read the beginning sentences. Then read the answer choices and put a check mark in front of **all of the sentences that are true** based on the beginning sentences. Remember that more than one answer is possible sometimes.

1. Jane and Libby went to the Smoky Mountains in Tennessee during spring break.
   ___ a. The Smoky Mountains are in Tennessee.
   ___ b. They went to Tennessee.
   ___ c. They went to the Smoky Mountains during spring break.
   ___ d. The Spring Mountains are in Tennessee.

2. Mario, Daniel, and Roberto watched *Titanic* at the Cineplex last night.
   ___ a. They watched *Titanic* at Daniel's house.
   ___ b. Tatiana went to the movies with Roberto.
   ___ c. Mario, Daniel, and Roberto went to a movie last night.
   ___ d. The Cineplex is a movie theater.

3. The final grammar exam is at 10:00 A.M. on Tuesday, December 7.
   ___ a. The final exam is in the morning.
   ___ b. The grammar exam is on Tuesday.
   ___ c. The grammar and listening examinations are at 10:00 A.M.
   ___ d. December is the seventh month of the year.

4. Chauncey's Steak House serves delicious barbecued steaks and all kinds of fresh seafood.
   ___ a. Chauncey's serves steaks and fish.
   ___ b. Chauncey's serves delicious food.
   ___ c. A great place for a steak is Chauncey's.
   ___ d. Fresh seafood is the only food served at Chauncey's.

5. There are some blueberry muffins on the table in the kitchen.
   ___ a. You can find the muffins in the kitchen.
   ___ b. The kitchen has a table.
   ___ c. The blueberries are in the refrigerator.
   ___ d. The kitchen table is blue.

6. A big gray cat lives in the little house on the corner.
   ___ a. The house on the corner is small.
   ___ b. The gray cat is big.
   ___ c. The cat lives in the gray house.
   ___ d. The big cat is gray.

7. The teacher's conference was in Birmingham, Alabama, November 11–13. She enjoyed it very much.
   ___ a. Birmingham is a city in Alabama.
   ___ b. The conference ended on November 11.
   ___ c. The conference was in November.
   ___ d. The teacher attended the conference.

8. We studied *wh-* questions in unit 7 of this book last week.
   ___ a. We studied unit 7 last week.
   ___ b. *Wh-* questions are in unit 7.
   ___ c. This is the last unit in this book.
   ___ d. We studied seven units in one week.

Exercise 7.   **TOEFL Review**

Part 1.   Completion. For items 1 through 8, circle the letter of the answer that best completes the statement.

1. My father ___
   a. works at a bank in Miami.
   b. works in Miami at a bank.
   c. in Miami works at a bank.
   d. at a bank in Miami works.

2. I have an appointment ___
   a. on Monday at 2:15 in the dean's office.
   b. at 2:15 in the dean's office on Monday.
   c. in the dean's office at 2:15 on Monday.
   d. at Monday in the dean's office at 2:15.

3. I live __

    a. on Lakeside Avenue in Ocean Park in a pink house.

    b. in a pink house on Lakeside Avenue in Ocean Park.

    c. on Lakeside Avenue in Ocean Park in a pink house.

    d. in a pink house in Ocean Park on Lakeside Avenue.

4. We meet for coffee __

    a. at Sebastian's at 7:00 A.M. on Tuesdays.

    b. on Tuesdays at 7:00 A.M. at Sebastian's.

    c. on Tuesdays at Sebastian's at 7:00 A.M.

    d. at Tuesdays on 7:00 A.M. at Sebastian's.

5. Paul and Ann had their honeymoon __

    a. at the Windjammer beautiful Resort in Hawaii.

    b. at the beautiful Windjammer Resort in Hawaii.

    c. in Hawaii at the Windjammer Resort beautiful.

    d. in Hawaii at the beautiful Windjammer Resort.

6. He wore __

    a. his new Italian suit yesterday to work.

    b. his suit Italian new to work yesterday.

    c. his new Italian suit to work yesterday.

    d. to work yesterday his new Italian suit.

7. My husband likes __

    a. very spicy Thai food.

    b. spicy food very Thai.

    c. Thai food very spicy.

    d. food very spicy Thai.

8. Jonathan listens to ___.

    a. music classical at night in his room.

    b. classical music at night in his room.

    c. classical music in his room at night.

    d. music classical in his room at night.

Part 2. Error Identification. For items 9 through 15, read each sentence carefully. Look at the underlined parts. Circle the letter that shows the incorrect part.

9. Putman's <u>on Fifth Avenue</u> sells very <u>expensive</u> jewelry, but you can find less <u>expensives</u>
            A   B   C

    earrings at Zane's <u>in the mall</u>.
                        D

10. We took a <u>short</u> cruise <u>in the Caribbean</u> last winter. We ate <u>food delicious,</u> but we <u>ate</u>
              A   B   C   D

    too much.

11. Alaska is an <u>unusual state</u>. The <u>summer days</u> are very <u>longs</u>, but the <u>winter days</u> are
                     A   B   C   D

    very short.

12. "What do you usually eat for breakfast <u>in the morning</u>?"
                                            A

    "I like <u>English muffins</u> with <u>strawberry jam</u>, and I like <u>blacks coffee</u>.
              B   C   D

13. I need to meet <u>my</u> teacher <u>at Monday</u> <u>at 2:00 P.M.</u> to discuss <u>my test score</u>.
                  A   B   C   D

14. I love my grandmother's <u>flower</u> garden <u>in the summer</u>. My <u>favorites</u> flowers are the
                            A   B   C

    <u>yellow</u> poppies and white roses.
     D

15. "Can I help you get ready for the <u>birthday</u> party?"
                                    A

    "Yes, please put <u>these plates blue</u> <u>in the backyard</u> on the <u>picnic</u> table.
                  B   C   D

Unit 9

Present Progressive Tense

Exercise 1. **Realia** Read the e-mail from Louise to her sister, Rosalie. Underline the correct forms of the verbs in parentheses.

```
To:     Rosalie@luna.cas.com
From:   Louise@luna.mom.com
Cc:
Re:     Hello!

Dear Rosalie,

     Hi! How are you? I'm at work now, and I ❶ (take, am taking) a little
break.  I ❷ (working, work) five days per week, and I'm very tired. I ❸
(like, am liking) my job, but sometimes I ❹ (am wanting, want) to take a
vacation. My boss ❺ (has, is having) a party tomorrow for the employees,
and everyone here ❻ (is looking, is lookking) forward to it.  You know how
it is; people are different when they ❼ (not working, aren't working).
     My family is fine. The kids ❽ (study, are studying) music this
semester, and they ❾ (is loving, love) it. My oldest son ❿ (prefers, is
preferring) art, but my youngest son ⓫ (is having,  having) a great time
playing the violin.  The problem is that he ⓬ (isn't practicing, no is
practicing). You know how kids are!
     Well, I should get back to work. Please write to me and tell me how
you ⓭ (doing, are doing).

                                        Love,
                                        Louise
```

Exercise 2. **Original Sentence Writing** Use the following words to write affirmative statements, negative statements, and questions in the present progressive tense if it is possible. Add capital letters as needed. Pay attention to the punctuation at the ends of the blanks to help you decide if you should write a statement or a question.

1. (listen) / I / to classical music / now

   _____ .

2. (play) / Fred / the drums / now

   _____ ?

3. (like) / Jennifer / vegetables / (neg)

   _____ .

4. (take) / you / piano lessons / this year

   _____ .

5. (know) / Elias / the alphabet / (neg)

   _____ .

6. (read) / Chris / a book / right now

   _____ ?

7. (dance) / Barry / with Marilyn / now / (neg)

   _____ .

8. (run) / Linda and I / around the block / right now

   _____ .

9. (shop) / Nina / with her sister / now

   _____ ?

10. (use) / Krista / a lot of garlic / when she cooks Italian food

   _____ ?

Exercise 3.   **Realia** Read this telephone conversation between a mother and
her daughter who is away at summer camp. Pay special attention
to the underlined phrases. If the phrase is correct, write C above it.
If it is incorrect, write X on the phrase and put the correct answer
above it.

Daughter: Hi, Mom. How are you?

Mother: I'm fine, honey. ❶ <u>Are you like</u> summer camp?

Daughter: Yes, it's okay, but ❷ <u>I miss you and Dad.</u>

Mother: That's understandable, sweetie. We miss you, too. What kinds of activities

❸ <u>you doing</u> at camp now?

Daughter: Well, we ❹ <u>swim, dance, cook, and exercise</u> almost every day.

Mother: Really? That sounds great! ❺ <u>What you did cook</u> last night?

Daughter: Last night ❻ <u>I was cooking</u> some spaghetti. It was delicious!

Mother: M-m-m! I want to have some spaghetti! How about exercise? ❼ <u>What</u>

<u>exercises do you do?</u>

Daughter: We ❽ <u>hike, jog, and climb rocks every day.</u> ❾ <u>I'm having fun,</u> but ❿ <u>I'm</u>

<u>wanting</u> to come home.

Mother: **⓫** <u>I'm knowing</u> you want to come home, honey, but try to be patient.

Daughter: I will be. I'll just remember that I'm coming home in two weeks. I guess I'll

see you then.

Mother: That's right. I'll see you in two short weeks. Good-bye!

Exercise 4. **Puzzle/Game** Look at the list of twelve verbs below. Circle the progressive (-*ing*) form of each of these verbs in the puzzle below. Be sure to look for vertical words, horizontal words, and diagonal words. Be sure to circle a word *only* if it is spelled correctly.

1. read		7. study
2. write		8. hug
3. stop		9. try
4. get		10. cut
5. sit		11. ring
6. sing		12. snow

S	T	U	D	Y	I	N	G	T	O	R
N	O	K	I	N	G	C	E	R	S	I
O	I	L	N	P	L	U	T	Y	I	N
W	N	Y	P	S	I	T	T	I	N	G
I	G	S	W	R	I	T	I	N	G	I
N	S	T	O	P	P	I	N	G	I	N
G	R	E	A	D	I	N	G	R	N	G
A	B	C	H	U	G	G	I	N	G	O

Exercise 5. **Dialogue and Conversation Practice** Angela is at work, and she calls her husband, Anthony, to see how things are going at home. Complete the dialogue below. Use the present progressive tense of the verbs in parentheses to help you.

Angela: Hello?

Anthony: Hi, honey. It's Anthony. How are you?

Angela: I'm fine, but some of the kids are having problems.

Anthony: Really? (they / do) ❶ _____ ?

Angela: Well, Joey (run / in the house) ❷ _____

_____ , and Marie (chase / him) ❸ _____

_____ .

Anthony: Oh, no! Where's Michael? What (he / do) ❹ _____

_____ ?

Angela: Michael's okay. (he / sleep) ❺ _____

_____ .

Anthony: Good. What about the baby? (she / sleep) ❻ _____

_____ ?

Angela: No. (she / eat) ❼ _____ .

Did I tell you Joey's friend is here? (he / play / in the kitchen)

❽ _____ .

Anthony: In the kitchen? Isn't that dangerous?

Angela: No, he isn't cutting anything. (he / sing) ❾ _____

_____ .

Anthony: Good. I'm glad to know everyone is okay.

Angela: When do you think you'll be home?

Anthony: (I / write a letter / now) ❿ _____

_____ , but I think I can be home before 6:00. I'll see you then.

Angela: Okay. Hurry home!

Exercise 6.   **Sentence Study**   Verb tense is very important because it helps us understand the information in the sentence. It tells us whether the action is something that happens all the time or repeats, something that is happening now, or something that happened already and is finished. Read the beginning sentences. Then read the answer choices and put a check mark in front of **all of the sentences that are true** based on the beginning sentences. Remember that more than one answer is possible sometimes.

1. Brian works for the police department.
   __ a. This action is true all of the time.
   __ b. This action is happening now only.
   __ c. This action is finished.

2. Charlie brought muffins home for breakfast.
   __ a. This action is true all of the time.
   __ b. This action is happening now only.
   __ c. This action is finished.

3. Nancy is cooking fried green tomatoes for dinner.
   __ a. This action is true all of the time.
   __ b. This action is happening now only.
   __ c. This action is finished.

4. Fred walked all the way to school.
   __ a. This action is true all of the time.
   __ b. This action is happening now only.
   __ c. This action is finished.

5. It rains in Florida in the summer.
   __ a. This action is true all of the time.
   __ b. This action is happening now only.
   __ c. This action is finished.

6. My sister's cat sleeps outside.
   ___ a. This action is true all of the time.
   ___ b. This action is happening now only.
   ___ c. This action is finished.

7. Kelly studied criminal justice for eight months.
   ___ a. This action is true all of the time.
   ___ b. This action is happening now only.
   ___ c. This action is finished.

8. Birds eat worms.
   ___ a. This action is true all of the time.
   ___ b. This action is happening now only.
   ___ c. This action is finished.

Exercise 7.　TOEFL Review

Part 1.　Completion. For items 1 through 8, circle the letter of the answer that best completes the statement or question.

1. *Jim:* "Is it raining outside?"

   Ann: ___

   a. No, it is.

   b. No, it isn't.

   c. No, it aren't.

   d. No, it's isn't.

2. "___ your sister coming to the movies with us?"

   "No, she has a doctor's appointment."

   a. Is

   b. Are

   c. Does

   d. Should

3. They like tennis. They ___ a match on TV right now.

    a. watch

    b. watches

    c. are watching

    d. is watching

4. This is my first time eating popcorn. ___ it!

    a. I'm loving

    b. Loving

    c. I'm liking

    d. I like

5. Aunt Patricia ___ a letter.

    a. writeing

    b. is writing

    c. writing

    d. writes

6. Do Chris and her husband ___ dinner every night?

    a. cooking

    b. cooked

    c. cook

    d. cooks

7. That girl is in my class, but I always ___ her name.

    a. forget

    b. am forgetting

    c. forgets

    d. am forgot

8. *Ryan:*   Is Charlie coming to dinner?

   Kyle: __

   a. No, he is.

   b. No, he's isn't.

   c. Yes, he's.

   d. No, he isn't.

Part 2.   Error Identification. For items 9 through 15, read each sentence carefully. Look at the underlined parts. Circle the letter that shows the incorrect part.

9. Jim and Oliver <u>are working</u> full-time at the university this semester. Jim <u>taught</u>
                        A   B

   history, and Oliver <u>is teaching</u> early British literature. They <u>like</u> their jobs.
                              C   D

10. Lee and Chris <u>are talking</u> to each other now. Lee <u>is speaking</u>, but Chris <u>no is listening</u>.
                        A   B   C

    She <u>is not interested</u> in what Lee has to say.
            D

11. John <u>is practiceing</u> piano. He <u>likes</u> to play, but he <u>doesn't like</u> <u>to practice</u>.
              A   B   C   D

12. The boy across the street <u>sings</u> often. He <u>is singing</u> every day when he <u>walks</u> to
                                    A   B   C

    school, and his voice <u>sounds</u> beautiful.
                                D

13. The bus driver <u>enjoys</u> his job. He <u>gets</u> <u>to talk</u> to people from all over the world.
                        A   B   C

    He <u>drives</u> now.
            D

14. I <u>am feeling</u> comfortable with my new friends. They <u>give</u> me advice, and they <u>help</u>
          A   B   C

    me when I <u>have</u> problems.
                    D

15. I <u>prefer</u> to talk to my mother because <u>I think</u> she <u>is understanding</u> me. I think my
          A   B   C

    father <u>doesn't understand</u> me.
                    D

Unit 10

Count vs. Noncount

Exercise 1. **Realia** This advertisement for C-U Better Eye Wear has eight nouns. Find the nouns and write them under the correct "count" or "noncount" column.

C-U Better

Choose from:

⇒ **Modern Styles**

⇒ **Tinted Glasses**

⇒ **Comfortable Plastic**

Ready in about an hour.
Very little time!
Save money when you
buy 2 pairs

Call 555-4343 for your examination now!

Count Nouns	Noncount Nouns

Exercise 2. **Original Sentence Writing** Read the following words and write sentences using those words. Choose the correct quantifier from the words in the parentheses. Make the noun plural if necessary. Use the correct verb tense and form. Be sure to add a period at the end of each sentence. Study the example.

example: I / have (neg)/ a new bike (a, some)

I *don't* have a new bike.

1. He / put (neg) / sugar / in his coffee (some, any)

_____

2. The boy / buy / candy / at the store / yesterday (some, an)

_____

3. I / have (neg) / pencil (a, some)

_____

4. They / have (neg) / milk (any, a)

_____

5. I / find / money / on the sidewalk / yesterday (a, some)

_____

6. I / have / problem / with my roommate (an, a)

_____

7. We / need to get / peanut butter / at the store (a, some)

_____

8. I / want (neg) / ice / in my water (an, any)

_____

Exercise 3. **Realia** Complete this phone conversation between Rita and her grandmother. Use *a, an, some, many, much,* and *a few.*

Grandma: Hello?

Rita: Hi, Grandma. I want to make your hot cucumber relish, but I can't remember the recipe. Can you tell me, please?

Grandma: Oh, let's see. First, you will need ❶ _____ medium size frying pan. Next, heat ❷ _____ oil in the pan.

Rita: How ❸ _____ oil do I need?

Recipe for: Hot cucumber relish
From: Grandma
  2 tsp. olive oil
  1 small red pepper - finely chopped
  3 green onions - sliced and white
      separated from greens
  2 medium cucumbers - cut in small cubes
  1 tbsp. lime juice
  1 tsp. honey
  2 tsp. fresh mint - chopped
  ½ tsp. salt

Grandma: About 2 teaspoons. Then add ❹ _____ chopped sweet red pepper.

And at the same time, add the white parts of ❺ _____ green

onions.

Rita: OK. How ❻ _____ sweet peppers and how ❼ _____

green onions?

Grandma: One sweet red pepper and 3 green onions will be enough. Sauté them for

2 minutes. Then add ❽ _____ cucumbers chopped into ¼ inch

pieces.

Rita: How ❾ _____ cucumbers?

Grandma: Two medium cucumbers should do it. Now sauté this mixture for another

3 minutes and then remove the pan from the stove. Now you're ready to add

the green part of the green onions. And for seasoning, use ❿ _____

honey, lime juice, fresh mint, and salt.

Rita: Got it. But how ⓫ _____ of each?

Grandma: I never measure them. I just guess. But if you need to know, the recipe calls

for 1 tablespoon of lime juice, 1 teaspoon of honey, 2 teaspoons of chopped

mint, and ½ teaspoon of salt.

Rita: Great. Is that all?

Grandma: Yes, that's it. Now remember to serve it while it's still warm. It is wonderful

on grilled meats.

Rita: I will remember. Thank you, Grandma. You're the best!

Exercise 4.　**Puzzle/Game**　Complete the following sentences with *any, some, many, much, a little, a lot,* and *a few*. After you complete each sentence, take the letter from each circle and write it on the line above the corresponding number. You will create a palindrome (a sentence spelled the same forward as backward). Two letters are done for you.

What did the first man say to the first woman?

$$\underline{\;\;}\;\underline{\;\;}\;\underline{\;d\;}\;\underline{\;\;}\;\underline{\;\;}\;\underline{\;\;}\;,\;\underline{\;\;}\;\underline{\;d\;}\;\underline{\;\;}\;\underline{\;\;}$$
$$\;\;1\;\;\;2\;\;\;\;\;\;3\;\;\;4\;\;\;5\;\;\;6\;\;\;7\;\;\;\;\;\;8\;\;\;9$$

1. May I have __ __ Ⓞ __ water?

2. How __ Ⓞ __ __ books do you have?

3. There are not Ⓞ __ __ students from Canada in our class.

4. Chinese people traditionally don't eat Ⓞ __ __ __ bread.

5. I only have __ __ Ⓞ __ __ __ space left on my hard drive.

6. I have a headache. I need __ __ Ⓞ __ aspirin, please.

7. There are __ Ⓞ __ __ cities that I want to visit.

8. There are Ⓞ __ __ __ of exercises in this book.

9. Maria brought me __ __ Ⓞ __ coffee from Costa Rica.

Exercise 5.　**Dialogue and Conversation Practice**　Sue and Bill are at the farmer's market. They see many fresh fruits and vegetables. Everything looks beautiful. Write a conversation among Sue, Bill, and the clerk. Sue and Bill want to buy many items, but they only have a little money ($3.50). Use *a few, some, any, many,* and *there are*.

Sue:　Wow! Look at all of those vegetables.

Bill:　Yes, and the fruit looks beautiful. Do you want to buy something?

_____

_____

_____

_____

_____

_____

_____

_____

_____

_____

_____

_____

_____

_____

_____

Exercise 6. **Sentence Study** Read the beginning sentences. Then read the answer choices and put a check mark in front of **all of the sentences that are true** based on the beginning sentences. Remember that more than one answer is possible sometimes.

1. My family eats watermelon twice a week in the summer.
   ___ a. We eat only one watermelon.
   ___ b. We eat watermelons for two weeks.
   ___ c. We don't eat watermelon in the summer.
   ___ d. We don't eat watermelon every day in the summer.

2. My mother bought a sofa, a chair, and a lamp for the living room.
   ___ a. She bought a chair only.
   ___ b. She bought more than one item.
   ___ c. She bought a bed and a closet.
   ___ d. She bought some furniture.

3. My brother ate two pieces of birthday cake, and I ate one piece.
   ___ a. My brother didn't get any cake.
   ___ b. My brother ate all of the cake.
   ___ c. I didn't get any cake.
   ___ d. I ate some of the cake.

4. Help, help! There are mice in the house!
   ___ a. There is more than one mouse.
   ___ b. There is only one mouse.
   ___ c. I am afraid of mice.
   ___ d. The mice are not in the house.

5. Mom used three cups of flour to make seventy-two cookies.
   ___ a. There are a lot of cookies.
   ___ b. "Flour" and "cookie" are noncount nouns.
   ___ c. "Flour" and "cookie" are count nouns.
   ___ d. "Cookie" is a count noun, and "flour" is a noncount noun.

6. There isn't much water in the river this year.
   ___ a. The water level in the river is high.
   ___ b. The water level in the river is low.
   ___ c. The river is almost dry.
   ___ d. The river is going to flood.

7. There isn't much bread left.
   ___ a. We need a loaf of bread.
   ___ b. There are a few slices of bread left.
   ___ c. We have too much bread.
   ___ d. The bread is bad.

8. Susan's twelve-month-old daughter, Sarah, already has several teeth.
   ___ a. Sarah is Susan's daughter.
   ___ b. Sarah is twelve months old.
   ___ c. Sarah doesn't have any teeth.
   ___ d. Sarah has only one tooth.

Exercise 7. **TOEFL Review**

Part 1. Completion. For items 1 through 8, circle the letter of the answer that best completes the statement or question.

1. I eat ___ banana for breakfast every morning.

    a. many

    b. a

    c. an

    d. much

2. Don't forget to buy ___ bread at the store.

    a. a

    b. a loaf of

    c. a piece of

    d. a few

3. "Do you have any gum?"

    "No, I'm sorry. I don't have ___ ."

    a. any

    b. a little

    c. some

    d. many

4. ___ many beaches in Florida.

    a. There is

    b. There are

    c. They are

    d. It is

5. "What did you get for your birthday?"

"My sister gave me ___ French perfume."

a. any

b. many

c. some

d. much

6. "Do you want to eat ___ of birthday cake?"

"No, thank you. I'm on a diet."

a. much

b. a

c. a little

d. a piece

7. "What are you cooking? Your house smells wonderful."

"I just took three ___ of bread out of the oven."

a. loafs

b. loaves

c. bags

d. few

8. "Good morning. This is the Ticket Center. Can I help you?"

"Yes, please. I need ___ information about the circus."

a. some

b. any

c. an

d. much

Part 2. Error Identification. For items 9 through 15, read each sentence carefully. Look at the underlined parts. Circle the letter that shows the incorrect part.

9. *Tom:* "I just moved to <u>a new house</u>. Where can I buy <u>a furniture</u>?"
                          A   B

   Sue: "There is <u>a furniture</u> store on Thirty-ninth Avenue <u>near the bank</u>."
                     C   D

10. *Boy:*   "Mom, I'm thirsty. Can I have <u>a soda</u>?"
                                                A

     Mom: "No, but <u>there is</u> <u>any milk</u> in the refrigerator. It is better for <u>your health</u>."
                          B   C   D

11. It takes <u>35 cent</u> to make <u>a phone call</u>. You can use <u>a quarter</u> and <u>a dime</u>.
               A   B   C   D

12. Paul bought <u>a briefcase</u> and <u>a luggage</u> during the sale at Harvey's. He saved
                  A   B

     <u>a lot of money</u>. Now he is ready for <u>his</u> next business trip.
      C   D

13. We had <u>a little</u> rain yesterday. My garden really needed <u>much</u> water. The <u>tomatoes</u>
             A   B   C

     are dying, but the <u>carrots</u> are doing all right.
                         D

14. There are <u>some</u> new <u>movies</u> at the theater, but I don't like <u>any</u> of them. I am saving
                A   B   C

     <u>a money</u> for a comedy.
      D

15. <u>There is</u> not <u>many</u> room in <u>an</u> airplane seat. If you have long legs, you should ask for
      A   B   C

     a seat on <u>the</u> aisle.
                D

Unit 11

Prepositions

Exercise 1. **Realia** Look at the following advertisement for an insect spray. Fill in the missing prepositions.

Now available **①** ___ stores! The incredible **BUGZAP SPRAY!**

Insects are common, especially **②** ___ the summer. With **BUGZAP,** you can

kill bugs everywhere! **BUGZAP** kills the bugs **③** ___ your garden and home.

Our special formula works **④** ___ the morning and **⑤** ___ night.

Here is what one happy customer says . . .

"I had so many bugs **⑥** ___ home! With **BUGZAP** it was easy. I just sprayed

some BUGZAP **⑦** ___ 7 o'clock **⑧** ___ a Sunday morning,

and by noon, the bugs were gone."

Try **BUGZAP** and say good-bye to all your insect problems.

Exercise 2. **Original Sentence Writing** Read the following words and write sentences using those words. You may have to change some word forms and add prepositions. Be sure to add a period at the end of each sentence.

1. I / live / 1457 Elm Street

_____

2. My grammar class / begin / 9:00 / and end / 10:00

_____

3. My family / like / to take vacations / the summer

_____

4. This movie / end / midnight

_____

5. Bob / be / not / here. He / be / Pizza Hut

_____

6. I / born / May 26, / 1965

_____

7. The cherry blossoms / open / April / Washington, D.C.

_____

8. The new mall / be / Deerglen Drive

_____

Exercise 3.   **Realia**   Read the following letter from Jeremy to his friend Billy.
Underline the correct prepositions.

Dear Billy:
    How are you? How is everything ❶ (in/at)
Washington, D.C.? I'm fine, but I am really busy!
Let me tell you what is going on with me. First
of all, I got a new job ❷ (on /at) the mall.
It's not so interesting, but I love my schedule.
I work ❸ (in /on) Fridays, Sundays, and Wednesdays.
It's a part-time job because I am still in school
❹ (on /at) Regional Community College. I go to
work ❺ (at /in) 6 p.m. and stay until 10 p.m. I don't
have a problem working ❻ (in /on) the weekend
because you know I don't have many friends. I
saved some money, and I plan to come visit you
❼ (at /in) the summer. That's great, isn't it?
    I'm sorry I cannot write more. I have
to be ❽ (on /at) work soon. Please write me
back and tell me your news. I will try to
write you again soon.
                                Take care,
                                Jeremy

Exercise 4. **Puzzle/Game** Look at the puzzle below. There are eight prepositional phrases in the puzzle. Be sure to look across, down, and diagonally to find the phrases. Circle the eight prepositional phrases and then write them on the lines below.

at   1. _____

     2. _____

     3. _____

in   1. _____

     2. _____

     3. _____

on   1. _____

     2. _____

```
A T H O M E I X F O
O T R W A T N O O N
N I M O Q X T P M M
S R N I B R H M L Y
U W U N D O E A Q S
N P C M A D F B X T
D A O A Y P A K E R
A Q X Y Z R L Y N E
Y S T I P V L E W E
Z E P W O X R P S T
```

Exercise 5. **Dialogue and Conversation Practice** Theresa and Stella are friends. Stella has a friend (named Joey) that she wants Theresa to meet. Theresa wants to know some information about Joey. Write a dialogue (questions and answers) using at least six of the phrases below.

in January	on Wesley Street	at IBM	on Sunday	at 8 P.M.
in Chicago	in 1992	at home	at McDonalds	at the park
in the fall	at 6 A.M.	at midnight	on Elm Street	at work

Theresa: _____

Stella: _____

Theresa: _____

Stella: _____

Theresa: _____

Stella: _____

Theresa: _____

Stella: _____

Theresa: _____

Stella: _____

Exercise 6. **Sentence Study** Read the beginning sentences. Then read the answer choices and put a check mark in front of **all of the sentences that are true** based on the beginning sentences. Remember that more than one answer is possible sometimes.

1. Susan is in her living room.
   ___ a. She is in her house.
   ___ b. She is near her house.
   ___ c. She is not home now.
   ___ d. She is not in the kitchen.

2. The party begins at 9 P.M., and it's 7:30 P.M. now.
   ___ a. The party is on Saturday night.
   ___ b. The party begins 90 minutes from now.
   ___ c. A few people are at the party now.
   ___ d. The food and the music at the party were excellent.

3. Billy has a pain in his foot.
   ___ a. His foot hurts him.
   ___ b. Both of Billy's feet hurt him.
   ___ c. His shoes are very big. He needs to buy a small size shoe.
   ___ d. Billy is wearing white socks today.

4. Maria lives in Madrid now, but she worked in New York from 1998 to 2000.
   ___ a. She is in the United States now.
   ___ b. She is not in the United States now.
   ___ c. She worked in the United States in 1999.
   ___ d. She didn't work in the United States in 1999.

5. When he finished eating dinner, Sam put his dirty dishes on the counter next to the sink.
   ___ a. The dishes are in the sink.
   ___ b. The dishes are on the counter.
   ___ c. The dishes are dirty.
   ___ d. The dishes are clean.

6. The weather yesterday wasn't so nice, but today it is incredible. We had two inches of rain yesterday, but today it is sunny. The children are playing in the park.
   ___ a. The children played in the park yesterday.
   ___ b. It rained yesterday.
   ___ c. The children are inside now.
   ___ d. It is a great day to be outside.

7. I wrote the telephone number of the plumber on a small piece of yellow paper, and then I put it on the refrigerator. You can see it now.
   ___ a. The note is on the refrigerator.
   ___ b. The note is in the refrigerator.
   ___ c. The note is on yellow paper.
   ___ d. The note is in a yellow notebook.

8. Nina, Salina, and Rafaela are in class today. Their teacher is explaining something at the blackboard. Nina isn't paying attention, but Salina and Rafaela are.
   ___ a. The girls are at school.
   ___ b. The girls are not at school.
   ___ c. The teacher is at home.
   ___ d. The teachers are at home.

Exercise 7.   **TOEFL Review**

Part 1.   Completion. For items 1 through 8, circle the letter of the answer that best completes the statement or question.

1. Michael works as a manager ___ Billy Bob's Restaurant.

   a. at

   b. for

   c. on

   d. to

2. Can you meet me ___?

   a. in Monday

   b. on noon

   c. at 7:00

   d. for 7:15

3. Did you live ___?

   a. at Spain

   b. on Spain

   c. Spain

   d. in Spain

4. I don't see Ronald. He is probably ___ .

    a. in the home

    b. at home

    c. on home

    d. in home

5. The weather in Florida gets a little bit cool ___ .

    a. winter

    b. in the winter

    c. at the winter

    d. on the winter

6. We received our textbooks ___ of class.

    a. in the first day

    b. on the first day

    c. at the first day

    d. first day

7. The Coliseum is ___ .

    a. in Rome

    b. Rome

    c. at Rome

    d. on Rome

8. Julius is not home now. He is at the library on ___ .

    a. noon

    b. March

    c. 2395 Hudson Street

    d. Hudson Street

Part 2. Error Identification. For items 9 through 15, read each sentence carefully. Look at the underlined parts. Circle the letter that shows the incorrect part of the sentence.

9. <u>Does</u> Michelle <u>works</u> <u>at</u> Worldwide Travel <u>Agency</u>?
   A   B   C   D

10. Daniel <u>came</u> home for <u>dinner</u> <u>on</u> 7:30 last <u>night</u>.
            A   B   C   D

11. <u>The</u> kittens <u>are</u> <u>in</u> a small basket <u>at</u> the bedroom.
   A   B   C   D

12. Larry's <u>first</u> history <u>test</u> is <u>in</u> Monday, but his math text is <u>the</u> next day.
          A   B   C   D

13. <u>The best</u> pizza <u>on</u> town is <u>at</u> Lorenzo's Pizza Parlor <u>in</u> my neighborhood.
      A   B   C   D

14. <u>My</u> parents <u>come</u> to visit <u>me</u> last Wednesday <u>at</u> noon.
   A   B   C   D

15. I <u>put</u> your coat <u>on</u> the closet <u>in</u> the back <u>bedroom</u>.
      A   B   C   D

Unit 12
Review

Exercise 1. **Realia** Maria doesn't feel well, and she wants to make an appointment to visit her doctor. Fill in the blanks with the correct questions and affirmative or negative answers. Use the words in parentheses to help you.

Receptionist: Dr. Adelman's office. How may I help you?

Maria: Hello. I want to make an appointment to see the doctor.

Receptionist: Certainly, ma'am. (you / have / insurance) ❶ _____ ?

Maria: (affirmative) ❷ _____ .

Receptionist: (wh- / the name / of the insurance company) ❸ _____

_____ ?

Maria: It is V.I.P. Insurance.

Receptionist: (wh- / the insurance number) ❹ _____ ?

Maria: It is 76512-4.

Receptionist: Thank you. (wh- / you / want to see the doctor) ❺ _____

_____ ?

Maria: I want to see the doctor because I have a bad earache.

Receptionist: (wh- / the pain / begin) ❻ _____ ?

Maria: It began two days ago.

Receptionist: Okay. We can make an appointment for you. Are you available now?

Maria: (negative) ❼ _____ .

Receptionist: (wh- / you / available) ❽ _____ ?

Maria: I can come in later today.

Receptionist: Is today at 3:00 good?

Maria: (affirmative) ❾ _____ .

Receptionist: Okay. (wh- / your name) ❿ _____ ?

Maria: It is Maria Giansante.

Receptionist: Thank you, Maria. We'll see you today at 3:00.

Exercise 2. **Original Sentence Writing** Read the following words and write sentences using those words in the blanks. You may have to change some word forms. Write negative statements, *yes/no* questions, and *wh-* questions. Add capital letters as needed. Pay attention to the punctuation at the ends of the sentences to help you decide if you should write a statement or a question.

1. wh- / you / learn English

_____ ?

2. Abraham Lincoln / (neg) / the first president of the United States

_____ .

3. you / like / grammar

_____ ?

4. wh- / your birthday

_____ ?

5. The sun / (neg) / rise / in the west

_____ .

6. your parents / (be) / in this country

_____ ?

7. your father / cook / well

_____?

8. wh- / you / live

_____?

9. my sister and I / (neg) / like / to exercise

_____.

10. Yoko and Anna / (neg) / in class yesterday / (be)

_____.

11. Yoko and Anna / (neg) / in class today / (be)

_____.

12. wh- / your favorite actor / (be)

_____?

Exercise 3. **Realia** Read the letter Ikumi wrote to her parents in Japan telling them about her trip to a U.S. museum. Fill in the blanks with the best word in parentheses.

Dear Mom and Dad,

How are you? I'm fine. (This, That) ❶ _____ is a beautiful country. There are (much, many) ❷ _____ places to visit and (a little, a lot of) ❸ _____ interesting historical museums. I (went, am going) ❹ _____ to a museum last week. It (had, was having) ❺ _____ information about natural history. (That, Those) ❻ _____ museum was so great! I had (a lot of, many) ❼ _____ fun. I saw (any, some) ❽ _____ dinosaurs and I (touched, touch) ❾ _____ a live snake. The snake was (in, at) ❿ _____ a cage, but I was nervous anyway. (In, On) ⓫ _____ one room, I saw (some, any) ⓬ _____ dinosaur eggs that were millions of years old. We weren't allowed to touch them because they're very delicate. I hope everyone is doing well. I'll write again after my next adventure.

Love,
Ikumi

Exercise 4.   **Puzzle/Game** Read the clues for the crossword puzzle. Fill in the blanks and the answers in the puzzle.

Across

1. "_____ shoes are too tight!"

3. The past tense of *put* is

    _____ .

6. *Ann:*   "Where is the doctor?"

    Bob: "_____'s

    in the office."

7. "My books are _____ the

    table."

8. "I don't have _____

    money. I only have two dollars."

11. *Jill:*   "Were you nervous when

    you gave your speech?"

    Nolan: "_____ , I was!

    There were over one hundred

    people there!"

12. "I ate a huge breakfast this morning,

    _____ I didn't eat much at

    lunch today."

Down

1. I _____ my medicine before

    dinner.

2. There are _____ apples in

    the refrigerator.

4. Paul gave the books to

    _____ because he knows

    that we love to read!

5. _____ cats over there are

    very friendly.

9. Washington, D.C., is the capital of the

    _____ .

10. I _____ the bird singing

    outside.

13. They are very rich. They _____

    seven houses and three businesses.

15. We ate dinner _____ an ex-

    pensive restaurant.

Across

14. Nancy doesn't have many recipes.

    She only has _____

    _____. (2 words)

16. Louise _____ the tennis

    match on television last night.

Exercise 5.   **Dialogue and Conversation Practice**   Pablo is a college student. The dinner in his dormitory wasn't very good, so he wants to order a pizza. Complete the dialogue by writing the appropriate questions and answers in the blanks.

Pizza place:	Hello? Cheezy Louie's. How can I help you?
Pablo:	I'd like to order a pizza, please.

Pizza place:	Sure thing. ❶ _____ ?
Pablo:	I want mushrooms, onions, and olives on the pizza.

Pizza place:	❷ _____ ?
Pablo:	I want a medium pizza. Also, do you have sodas?

Pizza place:	❸ _____ .
Pablo:	Good. I would like a medium ginger ale.

Pizza place:	❹ _____ ?
Pablo:	No, I don't want anything else.

Pizza place:	❺ _____ ?
Pablo:	It is 12101 North Dale Mabry.

Pizza place:	Is that a house or an apartment?
Pablo:	It is an apartment.
Pizza place:	❻ _____ ?
Pablo:	It's apartment number 21.
Pizza place:	Okay. ❼ _____ ?
Pablo:	It's 555-5963. When will the pizza be here?
Pizza place:	The pizza will be there in thirty minutes.
Pablo:	Do you accept checks?
Pizza place:	❽ _____ .
Pablo:	Great! Thanks! I'll see you in thirty minutes!

Exercise 6. **Sentence Study** Read the beginning sentences. Then read the answer choices and put a check mark in front of **all of the sentences that are true** based on the beginning sentences. Remember that more than one answer is possible sometimes.

1. *Jorge:* "When did you arrive in this country?"
   Cho: "I wanted to get here in June, but I had trouble with my passport, so I didn't get here until two months later."
   ___ a. Cho didn't want to leave her country.
   ___ b. Cho wanted to arrive in August.
   ___ c. Cho arrived in April.
   ___ d. Cho arrived in August.

2. *Charlie:* "Where does Ann Johnson live?"
   Seymour: "She lived on 180th Street until 1984. Then she moved to Orange Grove Drive."
   ___ a. Ann doesn't live on 180th Street.
   ___ b. Ann lives on Orange Grove Drive.
   ___ c. Ann lives on 180th Street.
   ___ d. Ann moved to 180th Street in 1984.

3. *Sue:* "I want to buy those shirts. They're very pretty."
   Ann: "Yes, they are."
   ___ a. Ann doesn't like the shirts.
   ___ b. Ann thinks the shirts are pretty.
   ___ c. The shirts are not near Sue.
   ___ d. The shirts are near Sue.

4. *Delmary:* "Where's Takumi?"
   Lin: "He played golf for two hours, and now he's reading a book."
   ___ a. Takumi isn't playing golf now.
   ___ b. Takumi read a book two hours ago.
   ___ c. Takumi is reading a book now.
   ___ d. Takumi is playing golf now.

5. *Terry:* "Who is your favorite singer?"
   Janet: "I don't like Brittany. I like Celine Dion."
   ___ a. Terry isn't a fan of Brittany.
   ___ b. Terry isn't a fan of Celine Dion.
   ___ c. Janet doesn't like Celine Dion.
   ___ d. Janet doesn't like Brittany.

6. *Nina:* "Why don't you exercise more often?"
   Nanette: "I don't have a lot of time. There aren't 25 hours in a day."
   ___ a. Nanette doesn't have enough time to exercise.
   ___ b. Nanette needs more time in her day.
   ___ c. Nanette has enough time to exercise.
   ___ d. Nanette doesn't need more time in her day.

7. *Fred:* "What do you want me to buy at the store?"
   Chris: "There aren't any bananas and we don't have milk, but I think there is enough bread."
   ___ a. Fred wants Chris to buy milk.
   ___ b. Fred doesn't have enough bread.
   ___ c. Chris wants Fred to buy bananas.
   ___ d. Chris doesn't want Fred to buy bread.

8. *Juan:* "Where did you put your suitcase?"
   Cheryl: "There wasn't any space in the closet, so it's in the living room on the sofa."
   ___ a. Cheryl put the suitcase in the bedroom.
   ___ b. Cheryl put the suitcase on the sofa.
   ___ c. Cheryl put the suitcase in the closet.
   ___ d. Juan put the suitcase on the sofa.

Exercise 7.   **TOEFL Review**

Part 1. Completion. For items 1 through 8, circle the letter of the answer that best completes the statement or question.

1. "Are you confused about grammar?"

   "No, ___ ."

   a. it isn't

   b. I'm not

   c. it doesn't

   d. I don't

2. "___ like to dance?"

   "Yes, I love to dance."

   a. Are you

   b. Is you

   c. Do you

   d. Is it

3. "Are you a student?"

   "___ ."

   a. Yes, I am

   b. Yes, I do

   c. Yes, I was

   d. Yes, I did

4. "___ go to school?"

   "I go to school in Florida."

   a. When do you

   b. Which do you

   c. Where do you

   d. Why do you

5. "___ movie we are watching is very exciting!"

   a. This

   b. That

   c. These

   d. Those

6. "I can't buy that car because I don't have ___ money."

   a. a few

   b. many

   c. a little

   d. a lot of

7. "Susan can't come outside now because __ ."

    a. she studies

    b. she's studying

    c. she studied

    d. she doesn't study

8. "I live __ Fowler Avenue __ New York City."

    a. in . . . on

    b. at . . . in

    c. on . . . in

    d. in . . . at

Part 2. Error Identification. For items 9 through 15, read each sentence carefully. Look at the underlined parts. Circle the letter that shows the incorrect part.

9. When my mother and I <u>went</u> to the movies, she <u>liked</u> the movie, but <u>I no like</u> it.
                      A   B   C

    It <u>was</u> too violent.
        D

10. I <u>met</u> my friend at school today and <u>say</u> hello to her. She <u>was happy</u> to <u>see</u> me.
        A   B   C   D

11. <u>Those</u> cake is very <u>expensive</u>. I <u>bought</u> two cakes <u>for</u> the same price last week.
       A   B   C   D

12. My brother <u>wanted</u> to take a vacation. He <u>didn't have</u> any money, so I <u>offered</u> to give
               A   B   C

    him <u>any</u>.
        D

13. Brett <u>washed</u> his car, <u>cut</u> the grass, and <u>cleaned</u> the house, so now <u>he is sleeps</u>.
          A   B   C   D

14. <u>In</u> April 15, 1912, the *Titanic* <u>sank</u> to the bottom of the sea. Many people <u>died</u> <u>on</u>
      A   B   C D

    that night.

15. My doctor <u>asked</u> me where the pain <u>was</u>, and I <u>tell</u> him it <u>was</u> in my shoulder.
           A   B   C   D

Answer Key

Unit 1

Ex. 1, p. 1: 1. am 2. is 3. are 4. are 5. are 6. is
7. are 8. am

Ex. 2, p. 1: 1. Mary is in Texas with her parents.
2. Thomas and Simon are cousins. 3. The teacher
is not here today. 4. Are the girls home from
school? 5. I am happy to be in this class. 6. Are
you from Morocco? 7. We are very hungry. 8. Is
your name Spanish?

Ex. 3, p. 2: 1. is 2. is 3. is 4. Are 5. Are 6. are 7. Are
8. is

Ex. 4, p. 3: 1. is, Bucharest 2. are, Pacific 3. is,
Madonna 4. isn't, the United States 5. is, Nile
6. are, Brazil 7. is not (isn't), Japan 8. are,
Canadian

Ex. 5, p. 3: Answers will vary.

Ex. 6, p. 4: 1. b 2. abcd 3. ac 4. bc 5. bcd 6. ab
7. c 8. a

Ex. 7, p. 5: 1. c 2. b 3. b 4. a 5. c 6. c 7. b 8. b
9. D 10. A 11. C 12. B 13. C 14. A 15. D

Unit 2

Ex. 1, p. 8: Part 1. 1. Frank needs blue jeans.
2. Frank doesn't need diapers. 3. Frank doesn't
need lipstick. 4. Frank needs an English dictionary. 5. The Martins don't need a radio. 6. The
Martins need a credit card. 7. The Martins need
baby toys. 8. The Martins don't need a bicycle.

Ex. 2, p. 9: Answers will vary.

Ex. 3, p. 9: 1. Yes, it does. 2. Yes, it does. 3. Yes, they
are. 4. No, it isn't. (OR: No, it's not.) 5. Yes, you
do. 6. No, it doesn't. 7. No, you don't. 8. Yes,
you do.

Ex. 4, p. 11:

Ex. 5, p. 11: Answers will vary.

Ex. 6, p. 12: 1. a 2. ad 3. ab 4. ab 5. ac 6. abcd
7. cd 8. acd

Ex. 7, p. 13: 1. a 2. d 3. a 4. c 5. d 6. a 7. a 8. b
9. B 10. D 11. C 12. B 13. D 14. B 15. D

Unit 3

Ex. 1, p. 16: 1. These 2. these 3. those 4. those
5. those 6. Those 7. those 8. Those 9. those
10. These 11. these

Ex. 2, p. 17: 1. Those are beautiful trees. OR Those
trees are beautiful. 2. This is an interesting book.
3. These are delicious peaches. OR These peaches
are delicious. 4. That is a lovely hat. 5. Those are
sick cats. OR Those cats are sick. 6. Are these
wet towels? OR Are these towels wet? 7. Is that
a wonderful song? 8. Is this a difficult course for
you? 9. Are those shoes very expensive? OR Are
those very expensive shoes? 10. Are these boxes
heavy? OR Are these heavy boxes?

Ex. 3, p. 18: 1. This 2. This 3. those 4. Those 5. that
6. that 7. That 8. Those

Ex. 4, p. 19:

Ex. 5, p. 20: 1. These are my parents. 2. These are
my uncles. 3. Those are my sisters. 4. That is my
brother-in-law. 5. Those are my brothers.
6. Those are my grandparents. 7. That is my
grandmother. 8. This is my cousin.

Ex. 6, p. 21: 1. bd 2. bc 3. ad 4. cd 5. cd 6. ab
7. a 8. cd

Ex. 7, p. 22: 1. b 2. a 3. c 4. b 5. d 6. b 7. a 8. c
9. B 10. A 11. C 12. A 13. D 14. D 15. D

Unit 4

Ex. 1, p. 25: 1. her 2. my 3. your 4. His 5. Your 6. their 7. Our 8. its

Ex. 2, p. 26: Names and places will vary, but possessive adjectives used are 1. My. . . . 2. Her. . . . 3. His. . . . 4. His/Their. . . . 5. Her/Their. . . . 6. Their. . . . 7. His/Her. . . . 8. His/Her. . . . 9. His/Her. . . . 10. Its. . . .(OR His. . . . OR Her. . . .)

Ex. 3, p. 26: 1. My . . . stereo 2. His . . . leather interior 3. Her . . . convertible 4. Our . . . air bags 5. Their . . . red 6. your . . . tinted windows 7. Its . . . leather

Ex. 4, p. 27: Step 1. 1. her 2. our 3. your 4. our 5. their 6. your 7. my 8. its 9. his 10. your Step 3. an envelope

Ex. 5, p. 28: Answers will vary.

Ex. 6, p. 28: 1. cd 2. bd 3. cd 4. ab 5. ac 6. ad 7. acd 8. abd

Ex. 7, p. 30: 1. b 2. a 3. a 4. b 5. d 6. a 7. b 8. d 9. D 10. A 11. B 12. D 13. B 14. C 15. A

Unit 5

Ex. 1, p. 33: 1. was 2. was 3. were 4. Are 5. aren't 6. was 7. was 8. were

Ex. 2, p. 34: Answers will vary.

Ex. 3, p. 35: 1. were 2. were not 3. are 4. is 5. was 6. were 7. Are 8. was

Ex. 4, p. 36: *Across* 2. was 4. is 7. is 9. are 10. was 12. was, was 14. were 16. is 17. was 19. is 20. was 21. was *Down* 1. was 3. is 5. was 6. is 8. was 9. was 11. is 13. was 15. is 16. is 18. is

Ex. 5, p. 37: Answers will vary.

Ex. 6, p. 38: 1. acd 2. cd 3. abcd 4. b 5. cd 6. a 7. c 8. a

Ex. 7, p. 39: 1. a 2. d 3. a 4. b 5. c 6. a 7. c 8. b 9. C 10. A 11. B 12. D 13. A 14. A 15. A

Unit 6

Ex. 1, p. 42: 1. watched 2. listened 3. played 4. learned 5. wanted 6. tried 7. didn't understand 8. explained 9. practiced

Ex. 2, p. 43: 1. Nora watched tennis on television. 2. Kurt didn't do his homework. 3. Did you mail the letter? 4. Jennifer ate the lasagna. 5. Elias didn't like the fish. 6. Did it rain last night? 7. The dog heard a noise outside. 8. I didn't sleep last night. 9. Did you understand the teacher? 10. We went to the beach yesterday. 11. Tyler bought vegetables. 12. Did you read this book?

Ex. 3, p. 44: 1. began 2. practiced 3. did 4. Did (she) think 5. Did (she) play 6. didn't think 7. went 8. bought 9. didn't help 10. spoke 11. told 12. gave

Ex. 4, p. 45:

Ex. 5, p. 46: 1. I went to a store. 2. I bought a shirt. 3. I chose a blue shirt. 4. I made a cake. 5. I read the directions. 6. Yes, I saw my parents. 7. My friends came over. 8. we ate lunch. 9. Yes, I spoke English.

Ex. 6, p. 47: 1. d 2. b 3. bcd 4. bcd 5. bcd 6. ad 7. abc 8. ab

Ex. 7, p. 48: 1. c 2. b 3. a 4. b 5. c 6. b 7. c 8. a 9. C 10. B 11. A 12. B 13. B 14. D 15. A

Unit 7

Ex. 1, p. 51: 1. What/Which 2. What 3. When 4. Who/Whom

Ex. 2, p. 51: 1. Which pen do you want? 2. Where did they go? 3. Why did you go home? 4. Who/whom did Lisa go to the park with? 5. What did you eat for breakfast? 6. When did Shelly get home? 7. Why did the students do poorly on the test? 8. Where were you and your sister last night?

Ex. 3, p. 52: 1. What 2. where 3. Why 4. Who/ Whom 5. What 6. Where 7. What 8. Where

Ex. 4, p. 53: 1. What is the Taj Mahal? 2. Where is the Coliseum? 3. Why is the Panama Canal important? 4. Where are the Great Pyramids? 5. When did the German people take down the Berlin Wall? 6. Who is Neil Armstrong? 7. What does "e-mail" mean? 8. When did Princess Diana die?

Ex. 5, p. 54: Answers will vary.

Ex. 6, p. 54: 1. bd 2. acd 3. bd 4. b 5. ab 6. cd 7. ad 8. ac

Ex. 7, p. 56: 1. a 2. c 3. d 4. c 5. c 6. d 7. a 8. d 9. A 10. B 11. B 12. B 13. C 14. B 15. B

Unit 8

Ex. 1, p. 58: 1. You go to the dentist at noon on Monday. 2. You have breakfast with Sally at the Country Inn at 9:30. 3. It is at 3:30 on Tuesday. OR Jane's dance class is at 3:30 on Tuesday. 4. You meet the realtor at 1432 E. Branson Street at 11:00. 5. You apply for a loan at Union Bank at 3:00. 6. You have a lunch meeting with Patricia Cole at the London Tea Room at 11:30 on Thursday. 7. You go to a movie with Paul at 7:00 Friday night.

Ex. 2, p. 59: Suggested answers for exercise 2. Placement of adverb phrases may vary. 1. I eat a hot breakfast at home on Sunday mornings. 2. I get up at 7:00 A.M. on Monday, Tuesday, and Wednesday. 3. Do you go to the beach in the summer? 4. Mrs. Gridley was in room 205 at General Hospital last night. 5. My cousin will be here in the morning. 6. Does he have a computer in his dormitory room at the University of Florida? 7. Laura and Larry like to eat breakfast at the Eggery on Fourth Street every Saturday. 8. Paul works on a cruise ship in the Caribbean during the summer.

Ex. 3, p. 60: 1. Midnight Sun 2. ancient glaciers 3. mighty brown bears 4. majestic mountains 5. tallest mountain 6. adventurous gold miners 7. famous Alaskan salmon 8. gray whales

Ex. 4, p. 60:

Adjectives

Ex. 5, p. 61: Answers will vary.

Ex. 6, p. 62: 1. abc 2. cd 3. ab 4. abc 5. ab 6. abd 7. acd 8. ab

Ex. 7, p. 63: 1. a 2. c 3. b 4. a 5. b 6. c 7. a 8. c 9. C 10. C 11. C 12. D 13. B 14. C 15. B

Unit 9

Ex. 1, p. 66: 1. am taking 2. work 3. like 4. want 5. is having 6. is looking 7. aren't working 8. are studying 9. love 10. prefers 11. is having 12. isn't practicing 13. are doing

Ex. 2, p. 67: 1. I am listening to classical music now. 2. Is Fred playing the drums now? 3. Jennifer doesn't like vegetables. 4. You are taking piano lessons this year. 5. Elias doesn't know the alphabet. 6. Is Chris reading a book right now? 7. Barry isn't dancing with Marilyn now. 8. Linda and I running around the block right now. 9. Is Nina shopping with her sister now? 10. Does Krista use a lot of garlic when she cooks Italian food?

Ex. 3, p. 68: 1. X; Do you like 2. C 3. X; are you doing 4. C 5. X; did you cook 6. X; I cooked 7. C 8. C 9. C 10. X; I want 11. X; I know

Ex. 4, p. 69:

S	T	U	D	Y	I	N	G	T	O	R
N	O	K	I	N	G	C	E	R	S	I
O	I	L	N	P	L	U	T	Y	I	N
W	N	Y	P	S	I	T	T	I	N	G
I	G	S	W	R	I	T	I	N	G	I
N	S	T	O	P	P	I	N	G	I	N
G	R	E	A	D	I	N	G	R	N	G
A	B	C	H	U	G	G	I	N	G	O

Ex. 5, p. 70: 1. What are they doing? 2. is running in the house. 3. is chasing him. 4. is he doing? 5. He's sleeping. 6. Is she sleeping? 7. She's (OR: She is) eating. 8. He's (OR: He is) playing in the kitchen. 9. He's (OR: He is) singing. 10. I'm (OR: I am) writing a letter now.

Ex. 6, p. 71: 1. a 2. c 3. b 4. c 5. a 6. a 7. c 8. a

Ex. 7, p. 72: 1. b 2. a 3. c 4. d 5. b 6. c 7. a 8. d 9. B 10. C 11. A 12. B 13. D 14. A 15. C

Unit 10

Ex. 1, p. 75: Count Nouns: styles, hour, pairs, examination. Noncount Nouns: glass, plastic, time, money

Ex. 2, p. 76: 1. He doesn't (OR: didn't) put any sugar in his coffee. 2. The boy bought some candy at the store yesterday. 3. I don't (OR: didn't) have a pencil. 4. They don't (OR: didn't) have any milk. 5. I found some money on the sidewalk yesterday. 6. I have (OR: had) a problem with my roommate. 7. We need (OR: needed) to get some peanut butter at the store. 8. I don't (OR: didn't) want any ice in my water.

Ex. 3, p. 76: 1. a 2. some 3. much 4. some 5. a few (OR: some) 6. many 7. many 8. some 9. many 10. some 11. much

Ex. 4, p. 78: 1. some 2. many 3. any 4. much 5. a little 6. some 7. many 8. a lot 9. some. Answer to riddle: Madam, I'm Adam.

Ex. 5, p. 78: Answers will vary.

Ex. 6, p. 79: 1. d 2. bd 3. d 4. ac 5. ad 6. bc 7. ab 8. ab

Ex. 7, p. 81: 1. b 2. b 3. a 4. b 5. c 6. d 7. b 8. a 9. B 10. C 11. A 12. B 13. B 14. D 15. B

Unit 11

Ex. 1, p. 84: 1. in 2. in 3. in 4. in 5. at 6. at 7. at 8. on

Ex. 2, p. 84: 1. I live at 1457 Elm Street. 2. My grammar class begins at 9:00 and ends at 10:00. 3. My family likes to take vacations in the summer. 4. This movie ends at midnight. 5. Bob is not here. He is at Pizza Hut. 6. I was born on May 26, 1965. 7. The cherry blossoms open in April in Washington, D.C. 8. The new mall is on Deerglen Drive.

Ex. 3, p. 85: 1. in 2. at 3. on 4. at 5. at 6. on 7. in 8. at

Ex. 4, p. 86:

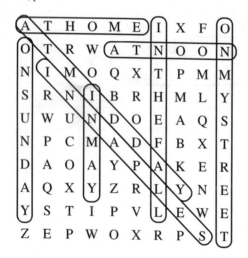

Ex. 5, p. 86: Answers will vary.

Ex. 6, p. 87: 1. ad 2. b 3. a 4. bc 5. bc 6. bd 7. ac 8. a

Ex. 7, p. 88: 1. a 2. c 3. d 4. b 5. b 6. b 7. a 8. d 9. B 10. C 11. D 12. C 13. B 14. B 15. B

Unit 12

Ex. 1, p. 91: 1. Do you have insurance? 2. Yes, I do. 3. What is (OR: What's) the name of the insurance company? 4. What is (OR: What's) the insurance number? 5. Why do you want to see the doctor? 6. When did the pain begin? 7. No, I am (OR: I'm) not. 8. When are you available? 9. Yes, it is. 10. What is (OR: What's) your name?

Ex. 2, p. 92: Answers may vary. Possible answers: 1. Why are you learning English? When did you learn English? Where did you learn English? 2. Abraham Lincoln wasn't the first president of the United States. 3. Do you like grammar? 4. When is (OR: When's) your birthday? 5. The sun does not (OR: doesn't) rise in the west. 6. Are your parents in this country? 7. Does your father cook well? 8. Where do you live? 9. My sister and I do not (OR: don't) like to exercise. 10. Yoko and Anna were not (OR: weren't) in class yesterday. 11. Yoko and Anna are not (OR: aren't) in class today. 12. Who is (OR: Who's) your favorite actor?

Ex. 3, p. 93: 1. This 2. many 3. a lot of 4. went 5. had 6. That 7. a lot of 8. some 9. touched 10. in 11. In 12. some

Ex. 4, p. 94:

Ex. 5, p. 95: 1. What do you want on it? 2. What size do you want? 3. Yes, we do. 4. Do you want anything else? 5. What is your address? 6. What's your apartment number? 7. What's your phone number? 8. Yes, we do.

Ex. 6, p. 96: 1. d 2. ab 3. bc 4. ac 5. d 6. ab 7. cd 8. b

Ex. 7, p. 97: 1. b 2. c 3. a 4. c 5. a 6. d 7. b 8. c 9. C 10. B 11. A 12. D 13. D 14. A 15. C